T0209116

国家汉办/孔子学院总部
Hanban/Confucius Institute Headquarters

Sima Qian

Collection of Critical Biographies of Chinese Thinkers

(Concise Edition, Chinese-English)

Editors-in-chief: Zhou Xian, Cheng Aimin

Author: Guo Weisen

Translators: Guosheng Yang Chen
Bo Ai

Expert: Zhang Jing

Nanjing University Press

《中国思想家评传》简明读本 - 中英文版 -

主 编 周 宪 程爱民

司马迁

著 者 / 郭维森 Guo Weisen

译 者 / Guosheng Yang Chen
Bo Ai

审 读 / 张 静

南京大学出版社

Editor: Rui Yimin
Cover designed by Zhao Qin

First published 2010
by Nanjing University Press
No. 22, Hankou Road, Nanjing City, 210093
www.NjupCo.com

Chinese Library Cataloguing in Publication Data
The CIP data for this title is on file with the Chinese Library.

ISBN10: 7-305-07294-9(pbk)
ISBN13: 978-7-305-07294-9(pbk)

《中国思想家评传》简明读本（中英文版）

编 委 会

主 任　许 琳　张异宾

副主任　马箭飞　周 宪

编 委　（按姓氏笔画为序）

　　　　马箭飞　王明生　左 健　许 琳　吕浩雪　张异宾

　　　　周 宪　周 群　金鑫荣　胡 豪　夏维中　徐兴无

　　　　蒋广学　程爱民

主 编　周 宪　程爱民

Editorial Committee

of

Collection of Critical Biographies of Chinese Thinkers

(Concise Edition, Chinese-English)

Executive Director: Xu Lin, Zhang Yibin

Associate Director: Ma Jianfei, Zhou Xian

Members of Committee: Cheng Aimin, Hu Hao, Jiang Guangxue

　　　　　　　　　　　Jin Xinrong, Lü Haoxue, Ma Jianfei, Wang Mingsheng

　　　　　　　　　　　Xia Weizhong, Xu Lin, Xu Xingwu, Zhang Yibin

　　　　　　　　　　　Zhou Qun, Zhou Xian, Zuo Jian

Editors-in-chief: Zhou Xian, Cheng Aimin

Books available in the collection

Confucius
《孔子》
978-7-305-06611-5

Laozi
《老子》
978-7-305-06607-8

Emperor Qin Shihuang
《秦始皇》
978-7-305-06608-5

Li Bai
《李白》
978-7-305-06609-2

Cao Xueqin
《曹雪芹》
978-7-305-06610-8

Du Fu
《杜甫》
978-7-305-06826-3

Zhuangzi
《庄子》
978-7-305-07177-5

Sima Qian
《司马迁》
978-7-305-07294-9

Mencius
《孟子》
978-7-305-07583-4

Mozi
《墨子》
978-7-305-07970-2

China is one of the cradles of world civilization, enjoying over five thousand years of history. It has produced many outstanding figures in the history of ancient thought, and left a rich philosophical heritage for both the Chinese people and the entire humanity. The fruit of these thinkers was to establish unique schools that over the long course of history have been continuously interpreted and developed. Today much of these thoughts are as relevant as ever and of extreme vitality for both China and the rest of the world. For instance, the ideal of " humaneness" and the concept of " harmony" taught by Confucius, the founder of Confucianism, have been venerated without ceasing by contemporary China as well as other Asian nations.

Ancient Chinese dynasties came and went, with each new dynasty producing its own scintillating system of thought. These rare and beautiful flowers of philosophy are grounded in the hundred schools vying for attention in pre-Qin times and the broad yet deep classical scholarship of Han and Tang times and in the simple yet profound occult learning of the Wei and Jin dynasties together with the entirely rational learning of Song and Ming Neo-Confucianism. The fertile soil of religious belief was Buddhism's escape from the emptiness of the sensual world and Daoism's spiritual cultivation in the search for identification with the immortals. The founders of these systems of thought included teachers, scholars, poets, politicians, scientists and monks—they made great contributions to such disparate cultural fields in ancient China as philosophy, politics, military science, economics, law, handicrafts, science and technology, literature, art, and religion. The ancient Chinese venerated them for their wisdom and for following moral paths, and called them sages, worthies, saints, wise men, and great masters, etc. Their words and writings, and sometimes their life experiences, constitute the rich matter of ancient Chinese thought distilled by later generations. The accomplishments of Chinese thought are rich and varied, and permeate such spiritual traditions as the harmony between humans and nature, the unification of thought and action, and the need for calmness during vigorous action, synthesizing the old and innovating something new.

Nanjing University Press has persisted over the last twenty years in publishing the 200-book series, *Collection of Critical Biographies of Chinese Thinkers*, under the general editorship of Professor Kuang Yaming, late honorary president of Nanjing University. This collection is the largest-scale project of research on Chinese thinking and culture undertaken since the beginning of the twentieth century. It selected more than 270 outstanding figures from Chinese history, composed their biographies and criticized their

中国是世界文明的发源地之一，有五千多年的文明史。在中国古代思想史上，涌现出了许许多多杰出的思想家，为中华民族乃至整个人类留下了丰富的思想遗产。这些思想成果独树一帜，在漫长的历史中又不断地被阐释、被发展，很多思想对于今天的中国乃至世界而言，仍然历久弥新，极具生命力。比如，儒家学派创始人孔子"仁"的理念、"和"的思想，不仅在当代中国，在其他亚洲国家也一直备受推崇。

古代中国朝代更迭，每一个朝代都有灿烂夺目的思想文化。百家争鸣的先秦诸子、博大宏深的汉唐经学、简易幽远的魏晋玄学、尽心知性的宋明理学是思想学术的奇葩；佛教的色空禅悦、道教的神仙修养是宗教信仰的沃土；其他如经世济民的政治、经济理想，巧夺天工的科技、工艺之道，风雅传神、丹青不老的文学艺术……都蕴涵着丰富的思想。这些思想的创造者中有教师、学者、诗人、政治家、科学家、僧人……他们在中国古代的哲学、政治、军事、经济、法律、工艺、科技、文学、艺术、宗教等各个文明领域内贡献巨大。古代中国人尊敬那些充满智慧、追求道德的人，称呼他们为圣人、贤人、哲人、智者、大师等。他们的言论、著作或被后人总结出来的经验构成了中国古代思想的重要内容，在丰富多彩中贯穿着天人合一、知行合一、刚健中和等精神传统，表现出综合创新的特色。

南京大学出版社坚持20余年，出版了由南京大学已故名誉校长匡亚明教授主编的《中国思想家评传丛书》，这套丛书共200部，是中国20世纪以来最为宏大的中国传统思想文化研究工程，选出了中国历史上270余位杰出人物，为他们写传记，

intellectual accomplishments; all in all, it is a rigorous and refined academic work. On this foundation, we introduce this series of concise readers, which provides much material in a simple format. It includes the cream of the crop of great figures relatively familiar to foreign readers. We have done our best to use plain but vivid language to narrate their human stories of interest; this will convey the wisdom of their thought and display the cultural magnificence of the Chinese people. In the course of spiritually communing with these representative thinkers from ancient China, readers will certainly be able to apprehend the undying essence of thoughts of the Chinese people.

Finally, we are deeply grateful for the support from Hanban/Confucius Institute Headquarters, and the experts from home and abroad for their joint efforts in writing and translating this series.

Editors
November 2009

评论他们的思想成就，是严肃精深的学术著作。在此基础上推出的这套简明读本，则厚积薄发，精选出国外读者相对较为熟悉的伟大人物，力求用简洁生动的语言，通过讲述有趣的人物故事，传达他们的思想智慧，展示中华民族绚烂多姿的文化。读者在和这些中国古代有代表性的思想家的心灵对话中，一定能领略中华民族思想文化生生不息的精髓。

最后，我们衷心感谢国家汉办/孔子学院总部对本项目提供了巨大的支持，感谢所有参与此套丛书撰写和翻译工作的中外专家学者为此套丛书所做的辛勤而卓有成效的工作。

编者
2009年11月

目录
Contents

Contents

Chapter I   Homeland, Childhood ------------------------------------- 1

Chapter II   Study Tour in His Twenties ------------------------------ 11

Chapter III From a Lang Zhong to a Prefect of the Grand Scribes ---- 23

Chapter IV   The Li Ling Affair Disasters ---------------------------- 41

Chapter V   The Historian after Corporal Punishment ------------ 51

Chapter VI   The Pinnacle of All Historians ---------------------- 65

Chapter VII The Lament Without Rhymes -------------------------- 99

Chapter VIII History to Last Forever   ---------------------------- 143

Translators' Notes --- 154

一 故乡，童年 ………………………………………… 1

二 二十漫游 …………………………………………… 11

三 由郎中到太史令 …………………………………… 23

四 李陵之祸 …………………………………………… 41

五 刑余的史臣 ………………………………………… 51

六 史家之绝唱 ………………………………………… 65

七 无韵之《离骚》 …………………………………… 99

八 光照千古 …………………………………………… 143

译后记 ………………………………………………… 154

一 故乡，童年

Chapter I   Homeland, Childhood

"Behold, the water of the Yellow River comes from the heavens above and runs to the sea without return." The Yellow River, like a dragon, winds its way across the land of China, nurturing the Chinese peoples. For thousands of years, civilizations emerged along the banks of it, and many wonderful stories abounded.

There is a mountain, the Dragon Gate Mountain (*Longmen* Mountain), which gets its name from the fact that it is shaped like an enormous gate spanning the river banks bordering Shanxi and Shaanxi Province. The legend says that the gate is a relic from many thousands of years ago when Yu the Great took over the hydraulic project in the area. Ancient records describe how the water rushes all the way from the upper stream and gathers here where the mountains make the water path narrow. When it comes to the Dragon Gate, it seems as if it is released and lets out a thunderous roar. There is another legend that goes with the Dragon Gate. Every year, the carp in the Yellow River would come and try to leap past the Dragon Gate. The successful carp would be transformed and become dragons that would fly up to heaven. The rest would stay in the water, with their failure marked on their foreheads. There are many other legends of the beautiful Dragon Gate area.

To the south of Dragon Gate, there was once, in the West Zhou Era, a city of military significance called Hancheng, the City of Han. The name was later changed to Shaoliang and again in 372 B.C. changed to Xiayang where the current city of Hancheng lies. In 145 B.C., the 5th Year of the Zhongyuan Period of Emperor Jing's reign in Han Dynasty, a boy was born in Zhichuan, Xiayang, into a Sima family. The boy was named Qian, with the style name of Zi Chang. This boy later experienced great suffering in life but he "did not give up his aspirations," and, against all hardship, compiled a great history book, the *Shiji*, or, *Records of the Grand Historian of China*, which contributed greatly to the development of humanity. He himself became a well known historian and literati in Chinese history.

Sima Qian loved his homeland and was very proud that relics of the well known hydraulic project of Yu the Great could be found there. In the "Postface" to the *Shiji*, it is said, "Qian was born in the Dragon Gate and later on took up grazing and farming between the area north of the Yellow River and south of the Mountain." When he said he was born in the Dragon Gate, he meant in the area, as it was a famous landmark. As for the Sima family's origin, they originated in Xiayang, where is the current city of Hancheng in

"黄河之水天上来，奔流到海不复回"。黄河像一条巨龙，蜿蜒奔流在古老中国的大地上，它哺育了伟大的中华民族。几千年来，在它的两岸产生过灿烂的文化，上演过许多可歌可泣的故事。

横跨黄河两岸，连着山西、陕西两省，有一座龙门山，形状就像一座雄关的大门。传说这还是大禹治水时凿开的。古书记载，龙门的气势是：两岸石壁矗立，大河被约束在山峡间盘旋，到了龙门这里，山峰忽然敞开，河水不再受约束，奔流而下，那声音就像无数的震雷在轰鸣！关于龙门，流传着许多神话，其中的一则说：大河里的鲤鱼每年都会聚集在这里，像比赛跳高似地往上游跳，跳过了龙门的，便化成神龙飞去，跳不过去的则在额头上留下失败的印记，还是退回去做鱼。龙门一带，风景壮丽，是产生过许多奇妙的神话传说的地方。

龙门以南，西周时代筑有韩城，是一处军事要地，后曾改称少梁，到了公元前327年更名为夏阳，地域相当于现在陕西省的韩城市。汉代景帝中元五年（公元前145年），夏阳的芝川地方，一家复姓司马的人家诞生了一个男孩，这男孩长成后，取名迁，字子长。他一生遭遇极其不幸，可是他"不欺其志"——也就是说忠实于自己的志向，忍辱负重，发奋著书，创作了《史记》这部伟大的著作，终于成为一位在人类文化发展史上作出卓越贡献的人物，成为中国历史上一位杰出的文学家和历史学家。

司马迁很爱他的故乡，并以故乡有大禹治水的遗迹而自豪。所以他在《史记·太史公自序》中说"迁生龙门，耕牧河山之阳"。就是说："我出生在龙门，曾在大河以北，龙门山以南耕种、放牧。"他说生在龙门，是因为龙门是当地的标志，就用来代指这一地区。要说司马迁的籍贯，当然应该说是夏阳，也

Shaanxi Province.

The grazing and farming activities in Sima Qian's childhood enriched his memories of his childhood and youth. He also said that, "at the age of ten, I could chant ancient scripts." That was one thing that he took pride in. The prevailing written style at that time was Li style. Since Sima Qian said he could chant the "ancient scripts," he must have meant that he was able to read the *Dazhuan*, an ancient style of calligraphy. Ever since the banning and burning of ancient books by the First Emperor of the Qin (*Qinshihuang*), not many such ancient books could be found. Without special tutoring, not many would be able to read the scripts. Sima Qian read such scripts, and he must have been able to access the national book collections because his father, Sima Tan, was Prefect of the Grand Scribes to the royal court. Sima Qian must have visited his father in the capital city of Chang'an and consulted the experts there. However, being able to chant the ancient scripts at the age of ten was still amazing. At the time of the Han Dynasty, there were two major types of schools, namely the current verse school and the ancient verse school. These two schools recorded classical works using different scripts and a lot of discrepancies existed between records, either in the records themselves or in the interpretation of them. According to the records, Sima Qian studied under Kong Anguo, the instructor of *the Book of History in Ancient Verse*, as well as from Dong Zhongshu, a master in current verse. Since Sima Qian had mastered the two verse forms and was able to use both of them, while compiling the *Shiji*, he collected texts in both verse forms and from different schools.

Not only was he proud of the fact that he was born in Dragon Gate, Sima Qian was also proud of the cultural tradition of his family. In the "Postface" to the *Shiji*, he traced his family origin to the time of Emperor Zhuanxu, one of the five emperors in ancient times. According to the legend, Emperor Zhuanxu assigned Nan Zhengzhong to be in charge of the heaven, and Huo Zhengli to be in charge of the earth. There are different legends about these two deities, but in essence, they were actually two grand sorcerers in charge of astrological observations and sacrificial ceremonies for mountains and rivers. The duties of these two were so closely related that they were often mentioned together. Later on, they were recognised as one. The name Zhongli became a name for a clan. In ancient times, the sorcerers were in charge of culture, and their interpretation of natural and social phenomena were authoritative. Society advanced and primitive religions were replaced by historical record-keeping. The time of the Culture of Sorcerers ended while the time of Culture of Historiography came into being. After some studies into the historical records, Sima Qian, basing his

就是今天的陕西省韩城市。

司马迁童年、少年时期在家乡从事过一些放牧、除草之类的农活，这给他少年时代的生活留下了美好的记忆。司马迁在《自序》中又说自己"年十岁则诵古文"，这也是他少年时代的得意事。所谓古文是指和当时通用的隶书不同的古代文字。既然诵读，那就应该是指用大篆古文写成的书籍了。秦始皇焚书、禁书之后，这种古籍保存很少，没有专门传授，也读不懂。司马迁十岁能诵古文，想必他也常到在首都长安任太史令的父亲司马谈那里，阅读国家藏书，向专家请教。他聪明好学，十岁就能诵读古文，毕竟是很了不起的事。汉代学术有今文、古文之争，对于传世经典，两大学派不仅记录的文字不同，解释也有许多分歧，所传授的解释经典的书籍也很不一样。据记载，司马迁曾向传授《古文尚书》的大学者孔安国学习过，也曾向今文经学的大师董仲舒求教过。因此，他是今古文兼通的，等到他写作《史记》的时候，他就将今、古文经来了个兼收并蓄，并不拘泥于学派的不同。

司马迁不仅以出生龙门自豪，同样使他感到自豪的，还有他极富文化传统的家世。《自序》一开始，讲自己家族的来历，便一直追溯到传说中的上古帝王颛顼（zhuānxū）时代。据说五帝之一的颛顼帝曾命南正重管理天，火正黎管理地。关于重、黎二位的神话传说纷纭错杂，大致这二位都是著名的大巫，掌管观察天文和祭祀山川的事，由于他们职掌的事密切相关，故而常常相提并论，后来竟合二为一，成了一个人了。也许重黎成了一个家族的称谓，故不再加以区分了。在原始社会里，巫又是掌管文化的人，他们是对自然、社会现象作出解释的权威。后来，社会进步了，原始宗教消歇了，巫便逐渐被史所代替，由巫官文化进入了史官文化的时代。司马迁根据一些古书

observations on some ancient recordings, identified that Zhongli was the ancestor of the Sima family, and as a result, he emphasised his family connection with the role of historians. In ancient times, historians were categorized as Celestial Officials, which means that they were officials in charge of astrological observations and calendar calculations. At the same time, "Left Historians record speeches while Right Historians record deeds," which means to record speeches of the rulers and major events in society was also the role of historians. The Zhongli family had been in charge of the roles of historians for many generations. In the Zhou Dynasty, when Xuan was the king, he appointed Xiu Fu, a Comte of the State of Cheng, to be the Grand Sima, leading an army to fight the barbarians in the Huai region. Xiu Fu would no longer serve as a Celestial Official, but he received the family name—Sima. Later on, the Sima family was able to take up the role of historians again before things changed in the middle of the Spring and Autumn Period. During the chaotic Spring and Autumn Period, the role of historians was abandoned, and the Sima family broke up and scattered. One clan, Sima Qian's ancestors, who had settled in Qin for many generations, stayed in Xiayang. Sima Cuo, Sima Qian's 8th generation great grandfather, was appointed to be the superintendent in the State of Shu because of his military achievements. Sima Jin, Cuo's grandson, a subordinate to Bai Qi who was a famous general in Qin, was recorded to have suicided with Bai Qi in Duyou, near Xianyang. Later on, Sima Chang, Jin's grandson, an official who came to be in charge of iron mines under Emperor Qin the First's reign. Sima Wuze, Chang's son, a Market Chief, was put in charge of the commercial markets in Chang'an. Sima Xi, Wuze's son, was never an official, but received a symbolic title of Wu Dai Fu, the 9th level military ranking out of 20. Xi's son was Sima Tan, Qian's father. In conclusion, their ancestors had served as historians in royal courts for generations. Sima Tan and Sima Qian had been mindful and proud of this fact and were determined to carry on their family tradition.

Sima Tan was appointed Prefect of the Grand Scribes in the early years of Emperor Wu's reign. The Grand Scribe was an official who received only 600 *dan*❶ of rice by way of salary, a rank equal to that of a Commandery Administrator. Despite this, the Grand Scribe was historically a Celestial Official like Zhongli. This was why Sima Qian had a line in his "Postface" which said "the Grand Scribe is in charge of the roles of a Celestial Official and is not in charge of earthly matters," which meant even though the Grand Scribes were in charge of heavenly matters, they did not actually have any power. Sima Tan was a well-educated person who studied astrology from Tang

的记载，确认重黎是司马这一姓氏的始祖，也就以此强调他史官家世的渊源。上古的史官，属于天官，主要职能还是观象授时，同时"左史记言，右史记事"，记录君主的言行和社会的大事件，也属于史官的职责。重黎一族，世代担任史官。到了周宣王时，有一位程国的伯爵叫做休甫的，被周宣王任命为大司马的官职去讨伐淮夷，不再担任天官的职务，但由此却获得了司马这个姓氏。后来司马氏又做了周王朝的史官，直到春秋中叶，才又有了变化。时代动乱，史职中断，司马氏一族也分散成了几支，在秦的一支世居夏阳，就是司马迁的嫡祖。司马迁的八世祖司马错在秦惠王时伐蜀有功，做了蜀郡守。司马错的孙子司马靳是秦国名将白起的部下，后来和白起同时被逼迫，在咸阳附近的杜邮自杀。靳的孙子司马昌，秦始皇时做过管铁矿的官。昌的儿子司马无泽，做过汉市长，就是管理长安部分商业市场的官。无泽的儿子司马喜没做过官，只有一个"五大夫"（二十级军功爵中的第九级）的空头爵位。喜的儿子司马谈，便是司马迁的父亲了。他们这一支，除司马错外，并不显赫，司马谈、司马迁念念不忘的，则是他们的先世曾经世代做史官，他们为此而自豪，并决心要予以继承、发扬。

汉武帝初年，司马谈担任了太史令。太史令级别不高，俸禄只有六百石❶，相当郡丞或州刺史一级。然而，从历史传统看，却是跟重黎一样的天官。所以司马迁在《自序》中还特别说明一句："太史公既掌天官，不治民"，这个职位管天不管人，说起来像回事，可一点权势也没有。司马谈是个很有学问的人，他曾向唐都学习天文，向杨何学《易》，向黄子学道论，而这三位都是当时著名的专家。司马谈写过一篇重要的学术论文——

---

❶ 石，中式容量单位，1石等于100升。

❶ Chinese unit of dry measure for grain (=100 litre).

Du, and studied *Yi* (*the Book of Changes*) from Yang He, as well as Daoism from Huangzi. These three people were all experts of that time. Sima Tan wrote a very important academic article, "Discussion of the Essentials of the Six Schools," which was recorded in the "Postface" to the *Shiji*. In his article, Sima Tan fully agreed with the Huang's teaching of Daoism. He criticised the other five schools, and at the same time he provided decent comments on them. His discourses were based on facts and were quite reasonable. Sima Tan thought that the fundamental teachings of the six schools all intended to put a good governance of the society, yet they had different methods of practice. Sima Tan's ambitions of carrying on the family tradition of being historians and the compilers of historical records had influenced Sima Qian greatly. Furthermore, Tan's collections and initial compilations were of great help to Qian's *Shiji*.

Sima Tan had long been coaching and tutoring his son to be his successor. He guided Qian in his studies. When Qian was 20 years old, Tan encouraged him to leave Chang'an for a long "study tour." The scholars in the past considered a study tour to be a very important way of self-cultivation and a means of development. To tour around and study had even become a custom. The reclusive poet Tao Yuanming, who lived 500 years later, wrote a poem which reads "when I was young and strong, carrying a sword I travelled on." Perhaps Sima Qian set out on his journey with a similar sentiment.

《论六家要旨》，现保存在《史记·自序》中。这篇文章全面肯定黄老学说，而对儒、墨、名、法、阴阳五家都是既有批评也有肯定。他的论述比较实事求是，合情合理。他认为六家考虑的都是治理好天下，只是所取道路不同，有得有失而已。司马谈的思想及其继承史官家世编撰史书的志愿，曾给司马迁以深刻的影响，他收集的史料和已写成的部分撰述，更给司马迁写作《史记》提供了很大的帮助。

司马谈给予他的儿子，也是他事业的继承人司马迁以悉心的培养，指导他读书、问学。在司马迁二十岁的时候，又鼓励他离开长安，作一次较长时期的漫游。古代的有志之士认为访学交游，作实地考察是非常重要的。游学甚至成了一种传统。五百多年之后，被称作隐逸诗人的陶渊明，也曾写过"少时壮且厉，抚剑独行游"。想必司马迁也是怀着这样的心情，开始了他的漫游。

屈原画像

Portrait of Qu Yuan

In 126 B.C., the 3rd year of the Yuanshuo Period of Emperor Wu's reign, a handsome young man was seen walking on the main road from Nanyang (currently Nanyang City, Henan Province) to Nanjun (currently Jiangling, Hubei Province). He was carrying simple luggage on his back. Whenever he came to a site of ancient war or of great historical importance, he would stop and observe. This young man was Sima Qian, a shining-star-to-be in Chinese culture and history.

Most likely Sima Qian had been influenced by his father, and he considered that knowledge from books would not be enough for the compilation of a great historical record. On-site investigations must be carried out in order to testify to the truth of the records in the books. Furthermore, accounts that were being passed down orally can be collected. With these aims in mind, Sima Qian departed from Chang'an. He went through the Wu Guan Gate, and from Nanyang he began his trip. He was 20 years old that year.

The journey was arduous but fulfilling. Sima Qian broadened his views, extended his knowledge and benefited a lot from it. The hardship was not a deterrent for such a knowledge-seeking energetic young man.

He crossed the Yangtse River (*Changjiang*) from Nanjun and came to the bank of the Miluo River, where the great poet Qu Yuan had terminated his own life about 150 years ago. The patriotic move of Qu Yuan, the truth-seeking poet, greatly moved Sima Qian. The waves of the Miluo River reminded Qian of Qu Yuan's poems, "The road ahead is winding and long, I would be seeking my path, no matter how hard it would be" and "As long as that is the truth I am longing for, I would not regret even if I were to die nine times." At this historical location, Qian shed tears. Now that Qian was in Changsha, one of the historic sites that was not to be missed out on was the old lodge of Jia Yi, a demoted politician who was dispatched to Changsha to assist the ruler there. Qian was greatly influenced by Jia Yi, a literati and politician. In "The Annals of the First Emperor of Qin" in the *Shiji*, Sima Qian quoted and fully agreed with Jia Yi's article "On the Errors of Qin." Jia Yi had proposed many political reform strategies and he was favoured by Emperor Wen of the Han. However

汉武帝元朔三年（公元前126年），从南阳（今河南南阳市）通往南郡（今湖北江陵）的大路上，走来了一位英姿飒爽的青年。这青年背负着简单的行囊，大步流星地赶路。但他逢到古迹遗址或是形势险要的古战场，便一定要停下来仔细考察一番，这青年不是别人，正是我国文学史、史学史上的巨星司马迁。

司马迁大概是听了他父亲的教导，认为要写出一部好的历史，光凭书本知识是很不够的，而必须作实地的调查，这样既能与旧有记载相印证，又能收集流传在人们口头上的活资料。于是，司马迁便抱着明确的目的，离开长安，出武关，取道南阳，开始了第一次漫游。这年，他刚满二十岁。旅途是辛苦的，但一路行来，开拓了眼界，丰富了知识，收获也真不小，这对求知欲旺盛的司马迁来说，真是幸福不过的事，受点辛苦，根本不在话下。

他从南郡渡江，来到长沙附近屈原自沉的汨（mì）罗江边。屈原，这位生活在司马迁之前一百五十多年，热爱祖国，向往光明的伟大诗人的事迹，深深感动了他。面对汨罗江的波涛，他的耳边仿佛响起了诗人的吟哦："路漫漫其修远兮，吾将上下而求索。"（路途多么漫长而遥远，我将上天入地去找寻。）"亦余心之所善兮，虽九死其犹未悔！"（只要是我心所向往的，哪怕死上许多次也决不后悔。）凭吊屈原的遗迹，他不禁流下了热泪。既然到了长沙，他当然也要寻访一下曾被迁谪为长沙王太傅的贾谊的旧址。这位汉初的文学家、政治家，给司马迁的影响也不小。《史记·秦始皇本纪》"太史公曰"的评语中，就全引了贾谊的《过秦论》，司马迁完全赞同贾谊的观点。贾谊年青时，受到汉文帝的赏识，提出许多改革政治的方案，但却受到守旧老臣们的强烈反对。文帝只好把他派到远离京城的长沙做王子的老师。后来始终没有得到重用，郁闷而死。（贾

his ideas were opposed by the conservative ministers in the royal court. The Emperor had no choice but to send Jia Yi to be the prince's teacher in Changsha, a long way from the capital Chang'an. Qian arrived in Changsha only 43 years after Jia Yi's death and it is likely that he could have found some valuable information.

In his famous poem "The Lament (*Lisao*)," Qu Yuan expressed his dream of crossing the Yuan River and the Xiang River and going further south in hope of meeting the spirit of Emperor Shun, the great sage, and confiding his grief. It was believed that Emperor Shun died on his trip to inspect the south, in the wilderness of Cangwu and was buried in Jiuyi Mountain (currently Ningyuan County in Hunan Province). The mountain has nine peaks and they look similar, hence was named Jiuyi, "Nine Doubts." After visiting Qu Yuan's death site, Qian wanted to have a look at the grave of Emperor Shun. He then "crossed the Yuan River and the Xiang River and saw the Jiuyi Mountain." Even though there were few relics for him to see, the mountains were worth seeing. Qian headed east after seeing Jiuyi Mountain and went to Lu Mountain (*Lushan*) to witness Yu the Great's legendary hydraulic project. Yu the Great was said to have dredged channels which later became Jiujiang, "Nine Rivers." Sima Qian examined the rivers and compared these to the legends. Qian then went downstream and arrived in Kuaiji Mountain (in currently Shaoxing, Zhejiang Province) and visited the famous Yu's Grotto, a deep hole where Yu the Great was buried. Legend has it that Yu the Great "spent 13 years away from home on the hydraulic project and did not return home even when passing by." When inspecting the Kuaiji areas, Yu the Great passed away there. He was buried in a very modest way by simply being wrapped in a bamboo sheet and put in a hole seven *chi* ❶ into the ground, not far away from a swamp. The locals, who benefited from his great hydraulic project, did not wish him to die and they turned him into a deity and the hole was named a grotto. Sima Qian looked upon Yu's spirit and paid his respects by visiting the grotto. Kuaiji had been the capital city of the State of Yue. However, Gou Jian, King of Yue was defeated and captured by Fu Chai, King of Wu. During his detainment, Gou Jian hung up a bitter gall bladder and licked it every day to remind himself of the shame so that he could revive his own state. From Kuaiji, Sima Qian went to Gusu in the State of Wu (currently Suzhou City). He climbed up Gusu Hill and looked at Lake Tai (*Taihu*). Sima Qian remembered all the historical events that had happened there. The arrogant Fu Chai, King of Wu, who listened to calumny and shied away from honest suggestions, ended up losing his battle with the revived Gou Jian. Fu Chai was cornered on the Gusu Hill and could not reach

谊的遭遇和屈原相似，他到了长沙，曾首先作赋悼念屈原，所以后来司马迁便将屈原、贾谊写成了合传。）司马迁到长沙时，距贾谊之死才四十三年，有关的遗迹是能找到一些的。

屈原在《离骚》中，曾幻想渡过沅水、湘水再往南走，去寻找古代圣君舜，向他倾诉不平。相传舜南巡死于苍梧之野，葬在九嶷山（在今湖南宁远县）。那山有九座山峰，峰峰相似，故称九嶷。司马迁凭吊屈原之后，便想去看一看舜的葬地。于是他"浮沅湘，窥九嶷"亲自到了那地方。古史遗闻已很渺茫，但山川形势还是值得一看的。从九嶷山折回向东，他登上了庐山，为的是看看茫茫九派（九条江河）如何汇合、分流，从而考察大禹疏导九江的传说。之后，他沿江东下，渡浙江，登会稽山（在今浙江绍兴），探寻著名的"禹穴"。所谓"禹穴"就是一个深洞。民间传说古代治水英雄大禹钻到这个洞里去了。大禹一生为人民治洪水，"居外十三年，过家门不敢入"，晚年东巡至会稽，死于此也就葬于此了。古书说他的墓地极简陋，是用茅草编的棺材，穿过水塘再下挖七尺❶就埋葬了。这样的人，人民是不愿他死的，故而造作了入于穴中的神话。司马迁对大禹治水的精神极为佩服，他"探禹穴"，也有凭吊一番的意思。会稽又是春秋时越王勾践的故都。勾践曾被吴王夫差打败，做了俘虏，假装完全臣服，得以回到会稽。他睡在柴草上，每天尝一尝苦胆，提醒自己不要忘记亡国的屈辱，艰苦奋斗，以求复国。这故事也是很动人的。司马迁游了会稽之后便由越而吴，登上姑苏山（在今苏州市），面对着烟波浩渺的太湖，古今多少兴亡事——涌上心头。金戈铁马，那骄横不可一世的

---

❶ 中式长度单位，1尺等于1/3米。

---

❶ Chinese unit of length (=1/3 metre).

an agreement with Gou Jian. Finally, he committed suicide there. While in the State of Wu, Sima Qian visited the site of the Palace of Huang Xie, who was also known as the Prince Chunshen of the State of Chu, one of four famous noblemen during the Warring States Period.

After Gusu, Sima Qian went to Huaiyin, home to the famous general Han Xin, who played a pivotal role in the war between the States of Chu and Han. Han Xin was very poor when young and was often bullied. Once, a few bullies stood in front of him and one said, "Hey, big man, even though you have a sword with you, you are a coward. Now, you either kill me with your sword or go crawling between my legs." Han Xin looked at him for a while and decided to do the latter. Actually, Han Xin was someone with great ambition. The story being told in the neighbourhood goes like this. Han Xin had buried his mother on high ground where people would come to live in the future. This signified that Han Xin would become a Marquis of Ten Thousand Households, meaning a high official in charge of a lot of people. Sima Qian went there and found the grave in the said location. In Huaiyin, there is another story, the story of the Laundry Lady who helped Han Xin. When Han Xin was young and had no job, a laundry lady supported him with meals every day. Han Xin was very grateful and said he would pay her back when he became rich. Hearing these words, the laundry lady told him off, saying, "I took pity on you because you, being a man, could not feed yourself. I never thought of receiving any remuneration from you." She had expected Han Xin to stand on his own feet and become a man. Her words were a great encouragement to Han Xin. This instructive story was recorded in the "Biographies of the Marquis of Huaiyin" in the *Shiji*.

From Huaiyin, Sima Qian travelled north and came to Qufu, the hometown of Confucius. Qufu was the capital of the State of Lu in ancient times. It was also a famous cultural city where ceremonial halls, carts, ceremonial dress and tools of etiquette of Confucius had been well preserved. The city was greatly influenced by the teachings of Confucius, to the effect that when a war broke out between Chu and Han and Liu Bang's army was in front of Qufu, the Confucian scholars were still studying the works of the classics, practising etiquette and music. Decades had passed, yet the tradition continued. This is why Sima Qian was still able to observe the etiquettes. Sima Qian had long looked upon Confucius as a great sage. While observing the practice, he thought about Confucius' image and was lost in thoughts of him. From there, Sima Qian went to Zou County, climbed up Yishan Mountain and inspected

吴王夫差，远贤信谗，最后反被勾践围困在姑苏山上，求和不得，只好自杀，悔恨莫及了。在吴地，司马迁还考察了战国四公子之一的楚国春申君黄歇的宫殿遗址。

离开了姑苏，司马迁便到了韩信的故乡淮阴。韩信，这位在楚汉战争中起了关键作用的大将，年青时十分贫苦。他曾被无赖欺侮，受胯下之辱。有一次，有几个无赖堵住他，说："大个子，你虽然带着刀剑，其实是个胆小鬼。你要不怕死，就杀了我，要是怕死，就从我两腿中间爬过去。"韩信看了他一阵，竟然从他胯下爬过。其实韩信是个胸怀大志的人。父老传说韩信把母亲葬在高旷的地方，以便将来能有万户人家在近旁居住，亦即意味着他预计将来要被封为万户侯。司马迁实地去看，果然如此。在淮阴还流传着漂母的故事。当年韩信贫穷挨饿，这位漂洗绵絮的劳动妇女，每天送饭给韩信吃。当她听韩信说将来要重重报答时，便很生气地回答说："男子汉大丈夫自己养活不了自己，我可怜你才供给你饮食，哪里希望你报答呢？"她完全出于同情心，丝毫没有想到接受报答，倒是很希望韩信能够振作起来，做一个自食其力的人。她的话对韩信是很大的教育与鞭策。后来，司马迁在《史记·淮阴侯列传》中特别写到这个故事，是有深刻意义的。

从淮阴北上，司马迁到了孔子的家乡曲阜。这里曾是古代鲁国的首都，是一座文化名城，孔子的庙堂、车服、礼器都还完好地保存着。这地方深受孔子影响，楚汉战争时，刘邦兵临城下时，鲁地的一些儒生，还在讲解诵读经书，演习礼乐，奏乐歌唱的声音一直没有断绝。几十年后，这种风习也没有改变，诸生还是定时来此习礼，让司马迁饱看了一番。司马迁对孔子是极为佩服的，他一边参观一边构思着孔子的形象，简直舍不得离开了。之后，他还到了邹县，登峄山，辨读秦始皇东巡时

stone inscriptions left by the First Emperor of the Qin. Sima Qian also experienced the Village Archery Ceremony taught by Confucius.

While taking his tour among those states and promoting his ideals, Confucius encountered difficulties between the States of Chen and Cai. Sima Qian experienced something similar in his travels. He said in the "Postface" that he also "encountered difficulties in Bo (currently Teng County), Xue (currently Xue City) and Peng City (currently Xuzhou City)." However he did not record the details of the difficulties. In the "Biography of Prince Mengchang," he said, "I have been to Xue, where I have seen some brutal young men. The local customs there were different to those in Zou and Lu." His explanation for the reason behind this was that this was the tradition of Shi-Keeping carried down from the Warring States Period. This might suggest there were some hooligans in Bo, Xue and Peng that had troubled Sima Qian. No matter what, the difficulties did not deter him from continuing his journey. He carried on from Peng City, the ancient capital built by King of Chu, and arrived in Pei County and Feng County.

Feng County and Pei County were the places where Gaozu of the Han and most of his ministers and generals came from. Gaozu, the first Emperor of the Han, and other famous heroes, were once commoners. Fan Kuai, for example, was a butcher, XiahouYing, a cart-driver for the county office, while Zhou Bo was a winnowing fan weaver, and a casual musician. No one would have thought these people would become what they became later. Furthermore, two prime ministers of the Han Dynasty, Xiao He and Cao Can, were lower ranking officials when taking part in the rebellion. Xiao and Cao were very afraid and did not want to lead the actions, so they recommended that Liu Bang take the lead. These insider stories could be found nowhere in the official history records. Sima Qian visited old people in the areas and befriended one of Fan Kuai's descendants, Fan Taguang, from whom he learnt some important information. Upon hearing this, Sima Qian's comment was, "Who would have thought?" He put this in the *Shiji*, and proved objectively the saying "Are those kings, dukes, generals and ministers born to be like that?" There are no so-called born saints and sages. Heroes are made by the times.

After staying in Feng and Pei for a while, Sima Qian went firstly to Suiyang (near current Shangqiu, Henan Province), and then arrived in Daliang (currently Kaifeng), the capital of the State of Wei during the Warring States Period. Qian couldn't wait to see Yimen, "the Gate of Yi," which is the Eastern Gate of Daliang, to collect information on a famous story, "Prince Xinling's famous story of Stealing the Commander's Tally to Save the State of

留下的刻石。在那里他还亲自演习了"乡射礼",认真体验了孔子所传的礼仪。

孔子周游列国时,曾在陈国、蔡国受困。司马迁在《自序》中说自己这次游历也曾"厄困鄱(今滕县)、薛(今薛城)、彭城(今徐州)",颇有点以孔子自命的味道。关于他如何受困,没有记载。不过在《孟尝君列传》中,他曾说:我曾经经过薛地,那里的里巷中多有横暴不驯的青年,风俗和邹、鲁大不一样。他将这原因归结为战国时养士的遗风。由此看来,他在鄱、薛、彭城受困,是受到暴徒的侵扰也说不定。困厄并没有动摇他继续漫游的决心。由楚霸王建都的彭城往西北,他便到了沛县、丰县一带。

丰县和沛县,是汉高祖刘邦及其手下许多文臣、武将的家乡。这些叱咤(chìzhà)风云的一时豪杰,原来都是些普通老百姓。樊哙原是个卖狗肉的,夏侯婴是个县衙门的车夫,周勃靠织"薄曲"(养蚕用具)过日子,有时还干干吹鼓手。这些人当老百姓的时候,谁也没有认为他们有啥了不起。汉初,先后做过丞相的萧何与曹参,当初也不过是沛县的小官吏,宣布起义时,他们还心存畏惧,不敢领头,因而才推举了刘邦。关于这些人的底细,官书家传中肯定是看不到的。司马迁访问了那里的父老,后来又和樊哙的削爵为民的后代樊他广结交了朋友,才得到这些宝贵的材料。面对这些材料,连司马迁也叹为"异哉所闻"了。他把这些材料组织进《史记》,客观上便足以说明"王侯将相宁有种乎",哪里有什么天生的圣贤,实在是时势造英雄啊!

在丰、沛逗留了一阵,司马迁经由睢阳(今河南商丘附近)抵达战国时魏都大梁(今河南开封)。为搜集信陵君窃符救赵的故事,他迫不及待地去参观夷门(大梁城东门)了。当年夷

Zhao." Wasn't it here where Hou Ying, the gate keeper, proudly mounted the cart driven by Xinling himself? Wasn't it here where Hou Ying bid farewell to Xinling and told him that he would take his own life upon Xinling's arrival at the army, so as to show his determination for their cause? Oh, Yimen, how many such moving scenes had you seen? How many speeches had you heard? It was a pity that the gate couldn't tell Sima Qian any stories, so he went to the citizens in the city for stories. Qian was seen under the wall of the city and along the main roads, asking locals there for historical facts. He was so sincere that people were very willing to tell him those stories he sought, either when they were enjoying a sun bath or taking a short break during labouring in the field. Qian listened and often recorded the stories using brush to mark on bamboo strips.

After visiting Daliang, Sima Qian returned to Chang'an.

The study tour had a great impact on Sima Qian's compilation of the *Shiji*. On the one hand, as Su Zhe, a famous literati of the Song Dynasty, pointed out, "the Grand Historian travelled around the country, saw all famous mountains and rivers in China, and befriended heroes in the Yan and Zhao in the north (currently Hebei and Shanxi Provinces). All these had contributed to the boldness of his style." On the other hand, many figures shown in the *Shiji* were so vivid and full of life. The stories were so rich in content that they could not be imaginary compositions written by Qian, nor could they have come from the royal collections in the gold caskets and stone chambers. Sima Qian gathered all this information during his study tour. His observations on the mountains and lands had greatly helped his writings on wars, on the benefits and harm done by water and flood, and also on the hydraulic projects.

His tour lasted about two years, covering around 15,000 kilometres. He went around nine provinces according to today's map. That includes Shaanxi, Hebei, Hunan, Jiangxi, Jiangsu, Zhejiang, Anhui, Shandong and Henan. After this tour, he was sent as an envoy to the southwest of the country. Later, he also accompanied Emperor Wu on his inspections which gave more chances for him to study the geography and people.

门监者侯嬴不就是在这里傲然登上信陵君亲自为他驾御的马车的吗？不也是在这里侯嬴送别前往救赵的信陵君，并告以当公子抵军时他将自杀以明不欺其志的吗？夷门啊！你看到过多少可歌可泣的行动，听到过多少慷慨激昂的话语！可惜夷门不能把这些告诉后人，那么只有向父老们访问了。于是在大梁的城墙边、大路旁，便不时可见一位青年，在向晒暖的、歇脚的田夫野老们恭恭敬敬地求教，还不时用笔和木简作一些记录。由于他谦虚、诚恳，父老们都愿意尽其所知地告诉他。

结束了大梁的访问，司马迁便回到了长安。

这次漫游与司马迁后来写作《史记》有很大的关系。宋代的文学家苏辙说：太史公巡游天下，遍览了中国的名山大川，和北方燕、赵（今河北、山西一带）英雄人物交往，所以他的文章开阔豪放，不同一般。指出了漫游对于司马迁散文风格的影响。这是一方面。另一方面《史记》中那许多栩栩如生的人物，生动丰富的故事情节，既不是太史公向壁虚构，也不是皇家金匮石室藏书所能提供。可以说大量材料都是这次漫游收集到的。对于山川形势的考察，对他写作战争史，研究水利、水害，论述水利工程，都有很大的帮助。

这次游历，时间约有二年，行程约三万里。按今天的区域，是跨越了陕、鄂、湘、赣、苏、浙、皖、鲁、豫九个省区。之后，他又曾奉使西南，多次随从汉武帝出巡，对山川、人物有了更多考察的机会。

司马迁注意搜集史料

Sima Qian Is Gathering Historical Information

After coming back to Chang'an, Sima Qian was chosen to join the royal court and became a Lang Zhong, Gentleman-at-the-palace, which was the lowest of the Lang Officials, "with salary of 300 *dan* of rice per year." (60 bushels received) Lang Officials were part of the emperor's retinue. Even though Lang Officials were of a lower rank, the fact that they were closer to the emperor provided them with more opportunities to be promoted. This was why many noble families and rich families liked their sons becoming Lang Officials for quick promotion. Both Sima Qian and his father were favourites of Emperor Wu, and they were able to accompany the emperor on his inspections. They were regarded as very fortunate.

Sima Qian's life had been strongly connected with Emperor Wu. To understand Sima Qian fully, it is best that we learn more about the emperor.

Emperor Wu, whose name was Liu Che, was born in 156 B.C., 11 years before Sima Qian was born. When Liu was enthroned, Sima Qian was only five years old. Emperor Wu could be regarded as one of the greatest rulers in Chinese history, having ability and wisdom. For the 54 years under his rule (from 140 B.C. to 87 B.C.), he scored many achievements. Relying on the economic strength built up during the 70 years' reign of his predecessors, and also relying on the foundation built by Emperor Jing, who suppressed the seven rebellious regions, Emperor Wu was able to strengthen the central control of the feudal society. He built up strong military forces and defeated the troublesome Xiongnu in the north. He also sent Zhang Qian as a special envoy to the Western Regions, cleared the path to the West and established the Han's control in the Western Regions. He also opened up the path to the "barbarous southwest." Ethnic groups in vast areas pledged allegiance to the Han. These groups included people from the west and the south of the current Sichuan Province, from the south of the current Gansu Province, and from areas in Yunnan and Guizhou provinces. He also conquered the forces in South Canton and Min, and unified large areas of China. While having wars externally, Emperor Wu carried out many huge hydraulic projects. He encouraged migration and land cultivation, and also developed many other industries. The Daoism theory of non-action was obviously no longer prevalent, and was replaced by Confucianism modified by Dong Zhongshu with some other theories, including the theory of the Disaster Revelations and the Circle of Five Elements. The feudal society was built upon the exploitation of the grass root peasants. Emperor Wu "used up the country's resources and lost half of its population" before scoring significant achievements in political, economic, military and cultural fields. In the middle period of Emperor Wu's

司马迁回到长安不久，便被选拔到朝廷里，做了一名郎中。这是郎官中最低一级，级别是"比三百石"（实俸六十斛）。郎官是皇帝的随从，职位不高，但因接近皇帝，容易受到提拔，所以贵族官僚、有钱人家的子弟，都积极谋求做郎官，以为进身的阶梯。司马迁父子二人都受到汉武帝的信任，随侍着武帝各地巡视，从当时的观点看，真是莫大的荣宠。

司马迁的一生与汉武帝有极大的关系，要了解司马迁，必须对汉武帝及其时代有个大略的了解。

汉武帝刘彻生于公元前156年，比司马迁年长十一岁，他做皇帝时，司马迁才五岁。汉武帝在历史上可说是一个"雄才大略"的统治者。在他做皇帝的五十四年（公元前140—公元前87年）中，确实成就了不少事业。他凭藉汉初七十年来积聚的经济力量，在景帝平定吴、楚七国之乱的基础上，加强了中央集权的封建专制制度。他建立了强大的军事力量，击败了不断侵扰中原的匈奴，又派张骞出使西域，打通了通往西方的道路，确立了汉朝在西域的统治权。又开通"西南夷"，使居住在今四川西部、南部，甘肃南部和云、贵地区的各族纷纷内附。还消灭了南粤、闽粤的割据势力，统一了广大国土。他在对外用兵的同时，对内又大兴水利，移民垦荒，兴办了不少事业。适应这时的形势，汉初主张的清静无为的黄老学说，显然是不适用了，代之而起的是经过董仲舒等改造过的，渗入了讲阴阳灾异和"五德始终"等内容的儒家学说。封建时代的大事业，是靠剥削压迫劳动人民来完成的，汉武帝统治时期，付出了"海内虚耗，人口减半"的代价，才取得了政治、经济、军事、

reign, frequent wars and extravagant life styles drove the Han economy to the edge of collapse. Various conflicts became more severe. In 107 B.C., the 4th year of the Yuanfeng Period of Emperor Wu's reign, there were about 2 million homeless people in the area to the east of the *Shanhai* Gate. During the Tianhan Period (100 B.C. to 97 B.C.), peasant uprisings took place in many places. To survive the financial crisis, the Emperor strictly punished mercantile profiteering, and also made salt-mining, iron-smelting, and coin-making stated-owned business. At the same time, he used methods of both suppression and pacification to control large-scale peasant uprisings. The Han Dynasty was exhausted by all these while political conflicts started within the ruling class. The Emperor, having noticed all these problems in his later years, issued an edict, "the Repentance Edict at Luntai," to acknowledge his errors, calling for a stop to wars and reducing compulsory public works. He issued policies that would benefit the people and appointed the Prime Minister to be a Fu Min Hou, a Marquis that Brings Good Life to the People. He also made Zhao Guo, an Agricultural Official, to be the Sou Su Du Wei, whose job was to be in charge of improving farming tools, farming systems and farming efficiency. By taking the above-mentioned measures, Emperor Wu was able to see some level of recovery in the social economy.

The era of Emperor Wu, on the one hand, was full of achievements; on the other hand, was full of ridiculous mistakes. The era provided Sima Qian with historical facts for the compilation of the *Shiji*. The ambitious, talented and totalitarian Emperor, who was also superstitious, had directly changed Sima Qian's life.

When Sima Qian was first chosen to be a Lang Official, it was at the pinnacle of Emperor Wu's achievements, both in the social, cultural and in military sense. At that time, Emperor Wu was busy making sacrificial offerings and inspections. After sacrificial offerings were made to the Five Emperors and Hou Tu, the Goddess of Land, he inspected the Henan and Luoyang districts and the western part of Gansu. He went to the Kongtong Mountain (West of Pingliang County in Gansu Province today) and he also inspected the area north beyond Xiao Pass (Xiaoguan, currently southeast of Guyuan County in Gansu Province) and had a huge hunting fair with thousands of his army in the Qinzhong area (currently the Hetao region in current Inner Mongolia). All these activities were for the purpose of demonstrating his military force, which served as a deterrent to the Xiongnu. Needless to say, when all these activities were happening, Sima Qian and his father were close to the emperor. In "The Annals of the Five Emperors," When Sima Qian said, "To the west, I've been to

文化各方面的巨大成就。武帝中期，频繁的战争和惊人的奢侈浪费，使得汉朝的经济濒于崩溃的境地，各种矛盾也都趋于尖锐。元封四年（公元前107年），关东各地约有二百万口流民无家可归。天汉年间（公元前100—公元前97年），广大地区都发生了农民暴动。虽然汉武帝采取打击工商业以及将盐、铁、铸钱三大利权收归国有等办法渡过了经济危机，同时又采用镇压与安抚的两手，制止了农民大规模的反抗，但是汉王朝毕竟大伤元气，统治阶级内部也出现了深刻的政治裂痕。这位皇帝晚年多少觉察到这种种问题，曾发布了著名的"轮台之诏"，公开承认某些错误，宣布要停止战争，减少兴作，实行富民政策。他封丞相为富民侯，起用精通农业的赵过为搜粟都尉，改良了农具和耕作制度，提高了生产效率。采用了这一切办法，终于使社会经济得到一定程度的恢复。

成就巨大而又充满谬误的汉武帝时代，为《史记》提供了现实的基础；既有雄才大略而又专制迷信的汉武帝本人，则直接影响了司马迁一生的道路。

司马迁开始做郎官的时候，正是汉武帝文治武功臻于极盛的时期。这时候，汉武帝正忙着祭祀和巡游。他祀"五帝"、祭"后土"，巡行河洛陇西，登崆峒山（今甘肃平凉县西），北出萧关（今甘肃固原县东南），与数万骑会猎于秦中（今内蒙古河套一带）。这些活动往往具有夸耀武力、震慑匈奴的作用。不用说，当他进行这些活动时，司马谈、司马迁父子都是随从

Kongtong," he was probably talking about Emperor Wu's visit to the Kongtong Mountain.

In 111 B.C., the second year after returning from Kongtong Mountain, Sima Qian was ordered by the emperor to inspect some ethnic groups in the southwest regions. This was a very important task. In order to "pacify the southwest barbarous areas," Emperor Wu had twice sent a great scholar by the name of Sima Xiangru. Sima Xiangru wrote two important essays: "On Ba Shu Xi" and "On the People of Shu." When Sima Qian was assigned the task as an envoy, five Initial Shires had already been set up. The people in these shires admired and wanted to learn the advanced culture and technology from the Han. And this was the reason why Sima Qian was sent there. Sima Qian went and turned his steps westward in the areas south of Ba and Shu. He went to the south in Qiong (currently Xichang County, Sichuan Province), Zuo (currently Hanyuan County, Sichuan Province), and Kunming (currently Qujing in Yunnan Province). By now, Sima Qian had been to all major places in Southwest China.

All emperors who had had great success would want to perform the Great *Fengshan* Ceremony; that is, a sacrificial offering ceremony to heaven on the top of Mount Tai, followed by a ceremony to the earth at the bottom of Mount Tai. All these ceremonies were carried out for the reason that whoever did this could claim to be the genuine Tian Zi, "Son of Heaven," who could have the legitimate right to do this. According to Guan Zhong, a minister of the State of Qi in the Spring and Autumn Period, the historical records suggested the number of rulers to have the Great *Fengshan* Ceremonies was 72, but he could only account for 12 by name. And those 12 could not be justified. Only one emperor, that is, the First Emperor of the Qin, after unifying China, performed the Great *Fengshan* Ceremony. There, the First Emperor of the Qin encountered great storm and had to hide under a pine tree. He later granted the title Wudafu Jue, "Marquis of the Fifth Rank," to the pine tree. It is a well-known story. Emperor Wu followed Emperor Qin's example in many areas and when his nation achieved utmost glory he naturally thought about the Great *Fengshan* Ceremony. In 110 B.C., the 1st year of the Yuanfeng Period, Emperor Wu led an army of hundreds of thousands of soldiers to the north and demonstrated his military power to the Xiongnu in the north. When he "returned, he made offerings to the Tomb of the Yellow Emperor at Qiaoshan, and he disarmed." Having done this, he had completed the preparation work for the Great *Fengshan* Ceremony. Sima Tan, being the Prefect of the Grand Scribes, was to participate in the ceremony and be in charge of the rites.

在侧的。在《五帝本纪》赞中，司马迁说："余尝西至空桐（崆峒）"，大概就是指随从武帝登崆峒山的事。

从崆峒回来的第二年（公元前111年），司马迁奉武帝之命去西南少数民族地区视察、慰问。这是一件很重要的任务。为"通西南夷"，武帝曾派大文学家司马相如两次去西南活动。司马相如还为此写过两篇著名的文章：《喻巴蜀檄》和《难蜀父老》。司马迁奉使的时候，西南地区已建立了五个"初郡"。这些"初郡"羡慕汉朝高度发展的封建文化，希望获得汉朝的先进技术。所以朝廷才派遣知识渊博、才华横溢的司马迁前去慰问。司马迁这一次往西到了巴、蜀以南，往南到了邛（今四川西昌县）、筰（今四川汉源县）、昆明（今云南曲靖），祖国的大西南几乎被他跑遍了。

据说，古代帝王凡建立了大功业的，都要举行"封禅大典"，就是先到泰山顶上筑坛祭天（封），再到泰山脚下梁父等小山上除地祭地（禅）。搞这个花样是为表示皇帝是货真价实的受命天子，有权祭祀天地和所有的名山大川。据春秋时齐国的大臣管仲说，历史上举行过封禅大典的有七十二君，但他能数得出的只有十二个。而这十二个也是极不可靠的传说。真正举行过封禅大典的只有统一了天下的秦始皇。秦始皇登泰山封禅，遇暴风雨，躲在松树下，因而赐给这棵松树以五大夫爵的故事是大家都知道的。汉武帝在许多地方效法秦始皇，国力达到极盛时，他自然也想到了封禅。元封元年（公元前110年）汉武帝亲率十几万大军，北巡朔方，向匈奴显示威力，"还，祭黄帝冢桥山，释兵须如"，搞了这一套，便完成了封禅的准备工作。身为太史令的司马谈，当然应随从封禅并参与制定礼仪的。可是走到周南（今洛阳附近），他生了重病，只好留下来。这时，司马迁从西南回来了，便赶来与父亲诀别。司马谈未能参

Unfortunately, when the procession came to Zhounan (near current Luoyang), Tan fell ill and had no choice but to stay behind. Sima Qian had come back from the southwest and rushed to see his father. It was a huge disappointment for Tan not to have participated in the Great *Fengshan* Ceremony. Holding Qian's hands, Tan cried with great disappointment, and he also encouraged his son to carry on the great work which he had started. Tan wanted Qian to continue the work of a great history book that would have a span from the Spring and Autumn Period to Han Dynasty. His words greatly influenced Qian and his work on the *Shiji*. Qian recorded it in "The Postface to the *Shiji*." After bidding farewell to his father, Sima Qian reported to Emperor Wu, who was in Shandong Province. Qian was allowed to participate in the Grert *Fengshan* Ceremony. We do not know Sima Qian's feelings during the ceremony. But later, he wrote a good article, "The Treatise on the Fengshan Ceremony," and included it in the *Shiji*. This article, a collection of Emperor Wu's ridiculous pursuits of eternal longevity, had a very obvious satirical tone. For example, Emperor Wu was deceived by Li Shaojun, an immortalist. The story was as amazing as one story in *Rulin Waishi*, "Anecdotes of Scholars." Besides, Emperor Wu's stubbornness was vividly described in the Shaoweng affair. A swindler by the name of Shaoweng was appointed Wencheng General. He fed to an ox a piece of silk with words written on it. He claimed that in the body of the ox there was a piece of holy script granted by Heaven. When the script was retrieved, the handwriting was recognised by Emperor Wu, and Shaoweng was executed. One would have thought the Emperor should have learnt his lesson from this. However, he encountered another person, Luan Da, who bragged about himself. When Luan Da was summoned by the Emperor, he said he dared not talk about shamanism because of the example of Shaoweng. The emperor said, "Don't worry. Go ahead and show me the secret of eternal longevity. Shaoweng died of food poisoning. He ate horse liver by mistake." The emperor was happy about Luan Da and granted him the title of Wuli General, but later had him executed because of his deceiving acts. And yet, despite this, another person who was like Luan Da was appointed to take the place of him. From "The Treatise on the *Fengshan* Ceremony," we can tell that Emperor Wu was really obsessed with the idea of immortality. He sent several batches of people to the ocean to find solutions for eternity but in vain, and yet he kept sending more and more people. After a long time without any results, he became tired of the words of the alchemists. However, he did not want to give up. He still hoped that one of them would be genuine in his abilities. He was like an addicted gambler who expected to be struck by luck. Sima Qian

与封禅大典，万分遗憾，他临死前拉着儿子的手，流着眼泪，嘱咐了一番话，除表示遗憾外，主要是叫儿子完成他未竟的事业，写出一部上继春秋，下迄汉代的好的历史著作来。这番话对司马迁影响非常之大，后来他郑重地写在《自序》中。司马迁诀别了父亲，便赶往山东向武帝复命，因此得以参与封禅典礼，他看到种种祭祀活动，当时他有什么感想，不得而知。不过，后来他写了一篇绝妙的《封禅书》编在《史记》里面。《封禅书》集中写了武帝种种愚昧的求仙故事，讥刺的用意十分明显。例如写武帝受方士李少君的骗，简直就和《儒林外史》中"侠客虚设人头会"一样精彩。写得最深刻的是汉武帝的执迷不悟。骗子少翁，官拜文成将军，他拿帛书喂牛，然后说牛肚里有天赐宝书。谁知武帝认得他的笔迹，一查，骗术败露，"文成将军"也被处死。照理说经过这件事，武帝应有所悔悟了。谁知他完全不觉悟，另一个骗子栾大又受到他的信用。这栾大的本事是敢吹大话，吹得连他自己都深信不疑。栾大初见武帝，吹了一通之后说：我害怕走上文成将军的老路，不敢再讲仙方了。武帝却掩饰说：文成将军是误食马肝中毒死的，你尽管贡献仙方吧。他心甘情愿地继续受骗。栾大被封为五利将军，后来也因骗术败露而被杀。可是又有一个骗子接替了他。从《封禅书》看，汉武帝确实是个神仙迷，他屡次派人入海求仙，没有效果，却更多地派遣，希望能遇到仙人。长久不见效，他对方士的胡话也有些厌倦，但还是舍不得抛弃，总想能碰上一个真有本事的。就像一个越输越赌的赌徒一样，他始终存在着侥幸心理。最后，司马迁用"自此之后，方士言神祠者弥众，

ended the article by saying "ever since, more practitioners came forward but the effectiveness was obvious for all to see." Sima Qian was faithful in recording historical deeds. He saw those superstitious actions of Emperor Wu and he wrote them down. Due to his own limitation, Sima Qian could not rid himself of his own feudalistic superstitious views either. However, his real life experiences had enabled him to appreciate truths and enabled him to write such an article of spirit of materialism.

One year after the Great *Fengshan* Ceremony, Emperor Wu, after listening to Gongsun Qing's words, went to Goushi and climbed up Mount Donglai to seek immortality. All he saw was a big footprint. At that time, there was a serious drought. Emperor Wu thought he had not achieved anything on his trip, so he changed his travel plans and went to inspect the Huzi Dam project (in the southwest of current Puyang, Henan Province), a huge hydraulic project. Back in 132 B.C., the Yellow River bank had broken here and flooded 16 shires. The river bank had not been thoroughly repaired for 20 odd years. Emperor Wu ordered Ji Ren and Guo Chang to repair the bank and they then ordered tens of thousands of peasants to work on the river bank. When he was there, Emperor Wu inspected the site and ordered a white horse and jade to be thrown into the river to pray. He then ordered everyone, apart from the general, to carry tree branches and straw to block the river. The magnificent scene inspired Emperor Wu. He wrote two poems expressing his genuine feelings, one of which goes, "Oh, River God, why are you so cruel? Oh, my people, how much grief you are experiencing because of the flood." However, he did not forget to write something to justify his Great *Fengshan* Ceremony and other sacrificial ceremonies. He said, "Without the Great *Fengshan* Ceremony, how could I go around to know the outside world?" This water project was successful. Sima Qian, who had studied rivers, lakes and the sea, knew the importance and the risks of water. He carried tree branches like others. He also heard Emperor Wu's poems and was greatly moved by the Emperor. He later wrote an article, "On Rivers and Canals," and put it in the *Shiji*. In the article he used the dredging of the Canal of Zheng as an example to emphasise the importance of building up the economic power of a country. At the same time, he disclosed the reason why the Prime Minister, Tian Fen, objected to this hydraulic project. Tian claimed that it was Heaven's intention that the river bank should break, and it was wrong to repair it. Sima Qian pointed out that Tian said so because the river flooded the south bank and he had a lot of lands on the north bank. Not repairing the broken bank was to Tian's advantage. Emperor Wu listened to

然其效可睹矣!"这句极妙的话结束了《封禅书》。司马迁是忠实于历史事实的,他亲眼目睹汉武帝种种荒唐的迷信活动,也就毫不含糊地记录下来。虽然,因时代的限制,司马迁自己在某些地方也未能彻底摆脱封建迷信思想,但是,生活实践使他看清楚了一些事情,写出了这样一篇具有唯物主义精神的名文。

封禅的第二年,武帝听信公孙卿的鬼话,到缑氏城,登东莱山求神仙,结果只看到一只大脚印,别的一无所获,那年又遇到旱灾,武帝也觉得出来一次没有成果,于是返回时便来到瓠子(今河南濮阳西南)塞河工地。这是一项伟大的水利工程。公元前132年,黄河在此决口,泛滥地区达十六个郡。决口二十多年一直没有很好治理。如今武帝命汲仁、郭昌等征发了好几万民工来堵塞决口。武帝亲临工地,先沉白马、玉璧祭河,然后便下令侍从百官,自将军以下,都得背柴草塞河。这样盛大的劳动场面,激发了汉武帝的诗情,他便作了两首著名的楚歌。其中有句云:"为我谓河伯兮何不仁,泛滥不止兮愁吾人!"形容河水泛滥的灾害,颇有感情。当然,在诗中他也没有忘记为自己劳民伤财的封禅、祭祀活动作一辩护:"不封禅兮安知外!"意思说: 不是来封禅怎么知道外面的情形。这次塞河导流工程是成功了。司马迁曾亲自考察过江、河、湖、海,深知水的利和害。他这次参加了背柴劳动,聆听了武帝的慷慨悲歌,也很激动。于是后来在《史记》中,便有了一篇《河渠书》。《河渠书》以郑国渠的开凿为例,强调了经济力量的重要。同时又揭露丞相武安侯田,因他的封地在河北,河决南口对他有利,便胡说什么江河决口都是出自天意,靠人力去

Tian's ridiculous words and did not have the project on for a long time. Sima Qian put all of this in writing and strongly opposed the theory of Heaven's intention.

In 108 B.C., the third year of the Yuanfeng Period, Sima Qian succeeded to the Prefect of Grand Scribes, as predicted by his father. The Grand Scribe had once been a very important position, and in ancient times was called the Celestial Official. The position became less important after the Zhou Dynasty. Historians were required to have expertise, and the title would be passed on from one generation to the next. The idea of carrying on the family glory had always been in Sima Qian's mind. In China, historians have the great traditional reputation of "no boasting and no covering up." For example, during the Spring and Autumn Period, Cui Zhu, a minister in the State of Qi, murdered King Zhuang. The Grand Historian of Qi recorded "Cui Zhu's regicided." As a result, the Grand Scribe was executed. The Grand Scribe's two younger brothers kept the same scripts and they were also executed. One other younger brother recorded the same message while another Grand Scribe was prepared to do the same. Cui Zhu, seeing that the threat of execution did not deter the actions of the Grand Scribes, had no choice but to let the script stay. There was another example. Zhao Dun, a minister in the State of Jin, often spoke out against Duke Ling, who hated him. Several times the Duke wanted to murder Zhao Dun but was not successful. Later, Zhao Chuan, one member of Zhao Dun's family, killed the Duke. Dong Hu, the Grand Scribe of Jin, in accordance with the "code of writing," recorded that "Zhao Dun committed regicide." Zhao Dun argued that he did not. The Grand Scribe said, "You are a minister. You were away at the time of the murder. However, you were still within the boundary of the state. When you returned, you did not punish the murderer. You can only be regarded as the mastermind behind this regicide." Zhao Dun could not argue any further. This was the " code of writing," a moral standard that did not distort the facts. This was the principle guarded by many historians with their lives. The excellent tradition had a great impact on Sima Qian, who realised the significance of the task of being a Grand Scribe and he was ready to devote all his life to it.

After becoming the Grand Scribe, Sima Qian started his preparations for the grand compilation. He read and sorted royal collections in the stone chambers and bronze caskets. At the same time, he had to follow Emperor Wu to visit places so he could not concentrate fully on his work. However, each visit he took with the Emperor broadened his views and increased his knowledge of society.

堵塞是不行的，去堵决口恐怕不合天意。武帝曾信了他的鬼话，长期没有去堵塞决口。司马迁记载了这一事实，可以说是对"天意说"的有力批判。

元封三年（公元前108年），司马迁继任太史令。这正是他父亲预见到的。史官在上古原是重要的职位，属"天官"，周代以来地位逐渐下降。但因史官需要专门知识，往往世代相传，所以前代的光荣往往在他们的耳畔回响，忠实于职务的传统往往能够得到继承发扬。我国古代史官是有着不虚美、不隐恶的光荣传统的。例如：春秋时，齐国大夫崔杼杀了齐庄公，齐国的太史便记录"崔杼弑其君"，崔杼便将太史也杀了；太史的两个弟弟继续这样写，又被杀。太史的另一个弟弟，同时还有另一位太史，又抱了竹简前往了。崔杼见杀不胜杀，只好由他们写去。再如晋国大夫赵盾，屡谏晋灵公，却招来了怨恨。灵公谋害赵盾不成，反为赵盾的家族赵穿所攻杀，晋太史董狐根据"书法"记载道："赵盾弑其君。"赵盾不服，进行申辩，太史说：你是正卿，出走并未离开国境，回来又不惩处凶手，所以只能认为你是杀死灵公的主谋者。赵盾没有话说，只好让他这样记录。古代良史的标准，就是"书法不隐"——不隐瞒事实。史臣们往往不惜以生命来保卫这一原则。古代史官的这种优良传统对司马迁有着深刻的影响，他自觉太史的责任重大，准备为之贡献出全部精力。

司马迁担任太史令以后，便开始阅读、整理石室金匮（国家藏书处）的大量资料，为《史记》的写作做准备。但这时他仍要随从武帝出巡，并不能集中精力写作。不过每次出巡，也都使司马迁扩大了眼界，增长了见识，加深了对社会的认识。

The first important task for Sima Qian to undertake was to participate in the correction of the calendar.

China has long been an agricultural country and has advanced knowledge of both astrology and the calendar calculation. Practical calendars were produced. During the Spring and Autumn Period, the calendar made was already comprehensive, and leap year system had been developed. During the Warring States Period, six different calendars (Six Ancient Calendars) were being used in different states, for example, the Yellow Emperor Calendar, Zhuanxu Calendar, Xia Calendar, Yin Calendar, Zhou Calendar, and Lu Calendar. These calendars were all Quarter Remainder Calendars, which means a year has 365 days and a quarter day in these calendars. However, each of these calendars set the beginning of the year on a different day. After the First Emperor of the Qin unified the country, he unified the calendars, too. He set the Zhuanxu Calendar as the norm and the beginning of the year to start in the month of *Mengdong*, "Meng Winter" (the 10th month according to the current Lunar Calendar). The Han Dynasty followed this calendar. (A bamboo calendar unearthed in No. 2 Silver Sparrow Tomb in Linyi, Shandong Province was the Zhuanxu Calendar. The bamboo calendar registered the year 134 B.C., the 1st year of the Yuanguang Period of Emperor Wu's reign.) The Zhuanxu Calendar, however, was not very accurate. After such long period of time, the calendar could not accurately match the celestial signs and there was a need for revision. At the same time, Emperor Wu, after performing the Great *Fengshan* Ceremony, linked the revision of the calendar with the "mandatory system reforms." According to the Cycle of Five Virtues, the nature of the Qin was the element of water, while that of the Han, a dynasty that defeated the Qin, belonged to the element of earth, which in nature blocks water. Once this theory was established, many systems of rites would have to be changed accordingly. No doubt this was a superstitious reaction. However, in ancient times, many developments in technology had to be disguised as superstition before it was acceptable. Being the Grand Scribe, Sima Qian had the mandate on astrology and calendars. He and Hu Sui proposed revising the calendar and started the project. They also recruited more than twenty known astrologists for the project, including Tang Du, Luoxia Hong, Deng Ping. Based on actual observations and detailed calculations, a new calendar was introduced. The introduction of a new calendar was an event of great importance and the title of the year, the 7th year of the Yuanfeng, was renamed the 1st year of the Taichu (Grand Beginning), which was 104 B.C. The Taichu Calender sets the 1st month on the lunar calendar to be the beginning of a year. It has 7 leap months

司马迁担任太史令之后，参加的第一件重要工作是修改历法。

我国自古以农业立国，故而早就有比较发达的天文、历算学，早就制定出比较合用的历法。春秋时历法已相当完整，已定出置闰的规则。战国时，各诸侯国历法不同，计有黄帝、颛顼、夏、殷、周、鲁六种历法，即"古六历"。这些历法都是以365 1/4日为一回归年——即"四分历"，但岁首（即一年开始的月份）不同。秦始皇统一中国后，用颛顼历，以孟冬（今阴历十月）为岁首。汉初沿用秦朝历法（1972年，山东临沂银雀山二号汉墓出土的汉武帝元光元年〔公元前134年〕的历谱竹简，正是颛顼历）。颛顼历不够精密，沿用既久，便产生了历法与天象不相适应的情况，因而有改正的必要。而举行过封禅大典的汉武帝则把改历和"受命改制"联系了起来。按"五德终始"的学说，秦为水德，代秦而兴的汉则应为土德。明确了这一点，许多礼仪制度都要作相应的变动。这当然是迷信，可是古代许多科学技术只有涂上一层迷信的色彩才被允许发展。司马迁身为太史令，天文、历法本是他职责之内的事。于是由司马迁、壶遂等建议开始了改历工作。当时还招募了民间历法家二十多人参加，其中包括著名天文学家唐都、落下闳、邓平等。在实测的基础上，经过精密的计算，一部新的历法完成了。修改历法是件大事，所以当时便将元封七年改为太初元年（公元前104年）。太初历以正月为岁首，仍用十九年七闰法，

in every nineteen years. And all leap months appear in the month where there is no middle-*qi* (one of 24 *qi* in solar terms in a year). This enables the harmony between seasons and months. The meeting of planets recorded on the Taichu Calender was more accurate than those recorded on the silks unearthed from Tomb No. 3 of *Mawangdui* (buried in 168 B.C.) of the Han Dynasty. It also calculated for the first time the cycle of the eclipse of the sun and the moon. These tremendous achievements could not have been possible without the hard work of Sima Qian and others.

When Sima Qian started to demonstrate his abilities, a huge misfortune fell on him.

但将闰月置于无中气（廿四节气，间分为节气与中气）的月份，使季节与月份比较适应。太初历计算的行星会合周期也比马王堆三号汉墓（葬于公元前168年）出土的帛书上的记述更为精确，并且还第一次计算了日、月食发生的周期。这些都是非常巨大的科学成就，这些成就的取得是与司马迁等人勤奋地工作分不开的。

正当司马迁奋发有为的时候，巨大的不幸降临到了他头上。

汉代砖画中的劳动场面
Labouring Scene from a Brick Painting of the Han Dynasty

李陵在劝苏武投降

Li Ling Is Inducing Su Wu to Capitulate

In the autumn of 99 B.C. (the 2nd year of the Tianhan Period), the leaves outside the Weiyang Palace started falling with the coming of the cool weather. However, the atmosphere inside the Palace was colder than the outside. Actually, it was not only the cold that was being experienced, to look at those ministers who shivered and sweated. They must have been experiencing the cold and the heat at the same time.

The news had just arrived that General Li Ling had surrendered to the Xiongnu, and Emperor Wu was furious. He had summoned his ministers to discuss the huge crime Li had committed.

Li Ling was the grandson of the famous general Li Guang. Li Ling had excellent horseback archery skills. He was a man of his word and he was not fond of monetary gain. He also had a good reputation. Emperor Wu had in the past sent him with 800 knights on a reconnaissance mission over 1,000 kilometres into the occupied areas of Xiongnu. Upon returning from the mission, Li was appointed to the post of *Qi Du Wei*, Commander of Cavalry, in charge of the frontier near Jiuquan and Zhangye with a troop of 5,000 brave soldiers. In early autumn of the 2nd year of the Tianhan Period, in order to create an opportunity for General Li Guangli, the brother of Emperor's favourite concubine, to obtain some military achievements, the Emperor sent him to Jiuquan with 30,000-strong cavalry to attack the Xiongnu. But Li Ling was ordered to be in charge of ordnance and supplies. Li Ling looked down upon Li Guangli, who used such connections to climb up to his post. Therefore when being summoned, Li Ling asked the Emperor's permission to take a troop to distract the enemy's armies. Emperor Wu was not happy about this suggestion and accused him of not wanting to be a subordinate to General Li Guangli. The Emperor also said that he had no cavalry to spare for him. Li Ling's reply was that he did not need cavalry but only 5,000 soldiers, and he could take the palace of Xiongnu— Chanyu Ting. Emperor Wu granted Li Ling's request, and also ordered Lu Bode, the Commander of Archery to be Li Ling's rear guard. Bode, who received titles as high as Billow-Subduing General, did not want to serve under Li Ling. He wrote and reported to the Emperor and said that autumn was not a good time to go to war with the Xiongnu as that was the season when their horses were strongest, and that it would be better to fight the following year in spring. He and Li Ling then could each bring a troop of 5,000 cavalry to attack Mount Junji from each side. They could catch Chanyu, the Xiongnu leader, with ease. Upon receiving the report, Emperor Wu was very angry, thinking it was Li Ling who regretted his own actions and asked Bode to report to him. The Emperor issued an edict to

公元前99年（天汉二年）秋天，未央宫前的桐树飘着落叶，天气转冷了。可是，未央殿里的气氛却比外面还要冷得多。不！那里不光是冷，有时又似乎很热。你看，那些朝臣们，一会儿瑟瑟发抖，一会儿又满头冒汗，心里正经历着严寒与酷暑。

因为这时，汉武帝刘彻听到李陵投降匈奴的败报，大为震怒，正召集群臣在这里议定李陵的罪行。

原来李陵是名将李广的孙子，精于骑射，讲信用，不贪财，有很好的声誉。武帝曾派他率八百骑兵深入匈奴二千余里，侦察了地形。回来后任骑都尉，率勇士五千人，在酒泉张掖一带，教射防边。天汉二年初秋时节，武帝为要让宠姬李夫人之兄贰师将军李广利立功封侯，便命李广利率三万骑兵出酒泉攻打匈奴，却命李陵替他管辎重。李陵实在看不起这位裙带将军，便在武帝召见时要求独当一面以分散敌人兵力。武帝大不高兴，说他是不愿隶属李广利，并说抽不出骑兵给他。李陵回答，不用骑兵，愿以所部五千勇士直捣单于廷。这样武帝便答应了他的请求，并命强弩都尉路博德为其后卫。路博德做过伏波将军，不愿为李陵后卫，于是便上奏说：现在秋天匈奴马肥，不宜与之交战，不如等到来春，我与李陵各领五千骑兵，夹击浚稽山，定可捉住单于。武帝看到这奏书十分生气，他怀疑是李陵后悔了，故意让路博德上奏。于是便下诏书给路博德，要李陵说明

Bode, demanding that he get an explanation from Li Ling, and at the same time, ordering Li Ling to set off with the army. Li Ling's army marched north from Juyan and reached Mount Junji. It was a smooth journey and Chen Bule was sent to the court to report the good news. Emperor Wu was happy and so were all the ministers at the court. No one knew that as soon as Chen Bule left, Li Ling's army was attacked by the main force of the Xiongnu. Chanyu, the Xiongnu leader, led a troop of 30,000 cavalrymen, which later increased to 80,000, and surrounded Li Ling's troops. Li Ling's army was very brave and they tried to fight their way out of the ambush to the south. There was a huge disparity in number between the two troops. Li Ling, ambushed and with no support, lost nearly all of his 5,000 soldiers, and in the end surrendered. Emperor Wu was shocked and furious when he heard this news. He called Chen Bule to account. Chen was cornered to commit suicide. The Emperor then summoned his ministers to the court to discuss Li Ling's crimes.

For some time after the ministers had arrived, none of them dared to utter a single word. Emperor Wu became even angrier, and turned his eyes on Gongsun He, the Prime Minister, "My Prime Minister, I' d like to hear what you say about it." Gongsun was a descendent of the ethnic "Hu" people. His wife was the elder sister to the Empress Wei. Because of this relationship, he had been twice granted the title of Marquis at different levels, and he was later promoted to Prime Minister from Grand Keeper of the Equipage. When the Emperor questioned him on this issue, he sweated immediately, and said, "In my humble opinion..." and then he realised that being a subordinate, he should not have any thoughts, and so he changed his words, "Your Majesty's view is very wise. Whatever my Lord decides will be the proper verdict." Emperor Wu had already known he wouldn't get anything out of this man. He sniffed and turned to Du Zhou, the Chief of Police. Du was an infamous, cruel official who was good at reading the Emperor's thoughts. He would persecute those who were being targeted by the emperor. He would also delay any trials of those the Emperor would like to have set free by mentioning that those people had been wrongly charged, so the Emperor could have an excuse to set them free. His motto was, the Emperor made decrees and his intention was the law. Du Zhou had known the Emperor's intention on Li Ling's crimes. Upon catching the eye of the Emperor, he bowed to the ground and said, "Your humble minister thinks that Li Ling has not lived up to the expectations of the Emperor and he has been arrogant. He has lost the battle and caused great humiliation to the country. His crimes are serious and he deserves to die. His whole family is as guilty as he is." These words were the words the Emperor had expected and a

一切，并催促李陵出兵。开始李陵军出居延，向北直抵浚稽山，行军顺利，便派部下陈步乐回来报捷。武帝高兴，朝臣也纷纷祝贺。谁知，陈步乐动身后，李陵便遭遇到匈奴主力。单于亲率三万骑，后来又增加到八万骑围攻他。李陵军英勇奋战，杀伤万余敌人，突围向南败走。但寡不敌众又被围困，矢尽援绝，五千壮士死伤殆尽，而李陵却投降了敌人。武帝得知消息，又惊又怒，立即责问陈步乐，逼得陈步乐自杀。随后便召集朝臣，廷议李陵的罪状。

皇帝升殿已经有一会儿了，可朝臣们面面相觑，谁也不敢先开口。武帝怒气更盛了，眼光射到了丞相公孙贺身上，说："葛绎侯，说说你的意见！"这公孙贺先世是"胡人"，他的夫人是武帝卫皇后的姐姐，所以他做将军虽无大功，却两次封侯，并由太仆而升任丞相。此刻武帝问到了他，他立刻出了一头汗，嗫嚅着回答："臣以为……"他立刻便觉得不妥，臣子是不该有自己的头脑的，便改口说："主上圣明，主上认为该判何罪是决不会错的……"武帝早料到这家伙讲不出什么意见，哼了一声便把目光转向执金吾杜周。杜周是个出名的酷吏，善于揣摩武帝的心思。凡武帝要打击的人，他便多方加以陷害，武帝要开释的人，他便迟迟不审问，却稍稍透露那人受了冤枉，让武帝有台阶可下。他的名言是：法令是君主定出来的，所以君主的意志就是法律！杜周此刻已摸透了武帝的意思，见武帝看他，便立即俯伏奏道："臣以为李陵辜负天恩，刚愎自用，丧师辱国，罪在不赦，其家属亦当连坐。"这几句话正是武帝愿

touch of a smile appeared on his face.

With two ministers taking the lead, other ministers, for example, Zhao Di, the Grand Minister of Ceremonies; Shang Qiucheng, the Grand Herald; Han Yue, the Superintendent of the Imperial Court; Wu ji, the Governor of the Capital and others, all followed suit and condemned Li Ling's crimes. Sima Qian, on the other hand, being a low ranking official, could only wait for all ministers to finish their comments before he could say anything. And, it was not necessary for him to make any comments on such occasions. However, because the emperor appreciated Sima Qian's artististic achievements, and he also wanted to know how this historian would write about this rebellious general, he asked Sima Qian's opinion. Sima Qian was sick of all the flattering comments from all the minsters who had been singing the praises of Li Ling only two days before and yet, were now condemning Li Ling. He thought: Li Ling, a loyal general, who had made such a proposition in order to solve the problems for the country, had done enough for the country. He may have made a mistake, but who would have thought these ministers could do what they had been doing? Sima Qian listened to their slanderous words and fabrications, and felt this was very unfair. He knew that both Li Guang and Li Ling were military geniuses, yet they had both experienced such misfortune. Upon all of these, when being asked by the Emperor, Sima Qian felt compelled to say something. Contrary to what all others did, Sima Qian sang Li Ling's praises highly. Li Ling was able to lead an army of 5,000 foot soldiers and fight with the whole of Xiongnu's army. He was able to fight his way for thousands of *li* ❶, and in the end, the situation was that there was no way out and there were no more supplies. Li Ling could have called on his soldiers to fight to the death. Even though Li Ling was defeated, his achievements were great enough to offset his failure. Furthermore, Li Ling might have surrendered, but he could have been surrendering in disguise, waiting for the right opportunity to show his loyalty to the Han Dynasty. What Sima Qian said was what the Emperor hated to hear. He became furious and retorted, "Are you trying to speak for Li Ling? Are you blaming General Er Shi?" General Er Shi was Li Guangli, who had led a troop of 30,000 cavalrymen and fought with King Youxian of Xiongnu. Li Guangli killed and captured around 10,000 Xiongnus but he also lost 60%— 70% of his soldiers. There was just no comparison between the two. The outraged Emperor ordered the guards to throw Sima Qian into gaol. During the long time of wars with the Xiongnu, there had always been surrenders on both sides, which had not overly disturbed the court. For example, Zhao Ponu, the Marquis of Zhuoye, who was defeated by and surrendered to the Xiongnu,

听的，他脸上掠过了一丝不易觉察的微笑。

这两个带了头，其他公卿大臣们，像新时侯太常赵第、大鸿胪商丘成、光禄勋韩说、京兆尹无忌等一批官僚，也就依样葫芦，都说李陵罪大恶极应重重治罪，等等。官阶很低的司马迁，只能靠边站，要等大家说完才有发表意见的机会。这种场合他是用不着讲话的。但武帝既欣赏其文才，又担心这颇不驯顺的史臣将来如何落笔，故而特意问到了他。司马迁眼见这批专会阿谀奉迎的官僚，前两天还奉觞上寿盛赞李陵的功劳，今天却又痛骂李陵，不给他留条退路，早就愤愤不平了。他想：像李陵这样的臣子，提出万死不辞的计划，为的是解救国家的急难，这已是很了不起的事情。现在一次失误，犯了过错，那些只知道保全自己、保全家庭的臣子，就立即说他的坏话，编造他许多问题，真是太不公平、太令人痛心了。他还想到李广、李陵祖孙都是奇才，但结局都这样不幸……骨鲠在喉，不得不吐。所以当武帝问到他时，他竟大唱反调，列举了李陵的种种优点，并说：李陵以五千步卒当匈奴举国之师，转斗千里❶，最后矢尽道穷，救兵不至；但李陵一呼劳军，其部下犹能振起作殊死战。虽失败，他的功劳也很不小了。再说李陵投降，也许是想要等待时机报答汉朝吧！司马迁的这番话击中了武帝的心病，只见他涨红了脸，高声斥骂道："你是为李陵做说客吗？是要诋毁贰师将军吗？"贰师将军就是李广利，他率骑兵三万与匈奴右贤王作战，斩、俘敌万人，而己方也损失了十之六七。与李陵一对比，优劣太明显了。汉武帝盛怒之下，立即命令廷尉将司马迁逮捕下狱。其实在汉朝与匈奴的长期战争中，投降过来、投降过去的事是很不少的。朝廷一般也不太追究。

---

❶ 中式长度单位，1里等于500米。

❶ Chinese Unit of length (=500 metres).

managed to return ten years later. He was still favoured by the Emperor. However, Li Ling's case was different. The subtlety behind this was that both General Er Shi and the emperor would be affected. They had been partly responsible for Li Ling's defeat. Sima Qian speculated that Li Ling "would seek the right opportunity and show his loyalty to the Han," but he was wrong. When Li Ling first surrendered, he was very remorseful. He had thought about learning from the example of Cao Mo from the Spring and Autumn Period, who coerced the Marquis of Qi to return the land of Lu. But Li Ling was disillusioned after Emperor Wu of the Han Dynasty killed his whole family. However, Li Ling did surrender and he confessed that "his crime was as so severe in nature that it would dash to the skies" when compared with Su Wu, the famous envoy who was kept by the Xiongnu for 19 years and had to herd sheep. Li Ling was sad and remorseful but he did not have any opportunity to "show his loyalty to the Han," which proved Sima Qian to be wrong. Sima Qian had to pay a tremendous price for his words. This is truly a great tragedy.

如浞野侯赵破奴战败投降，十年后逃归汉朝，武帝仍然信用他。可是对于李陵却决不宽假。这里的奥妙便在于牵涉贰师将军和武帝自己。李陵的失败，他们是都有责任的。司马迁推测李陵"且欲得其当而报汉"，也并非全无根据。李陵投降后，愧悔交集，是有学习春秋时曹沫劫盟迫使齐侯归还鲁地那样的想法的。后来，武帝杀了他全家，他才对汉朝绝望了。然而李陵毕竟是变节投降了，和奉使匈奴，拒不投降，不计一切个人恩怨利害，牧羊十九年终于归汉的苏武相比，他自己也说是"其罪通天"。他悲哀、愧悔，但实践证明，他终于未能"有以报汉"，因而司马迁的辩护也落了空。然而司马迁却为此付出了惨痛的代价，这真是历史的大悲剧。

汉代"瓦当"实物，上有"亿年无疆"四字
Eave Tile with the Four Characters" *Yi Nian Wu Jiang*" (Last
Forever) of the Han Dynasty

汉武帝画像

Portrait of Emperor Wu of the Han Dynasty

The moonlight came through the prison cell, casting light on the body of a 40-year old man with dark hair and dark beard. He sat there on the straw, motionless, like a statue made of iron. His bright eyes stared into the darkness, as if at some strange creatures that meant him harm.

Sima Qian was thrown into prison and bound hand and foot in chains. He was assaulted and abused by the jailers and he was scared all the time. When faced with such bullying, he thought about death many times. However, he still had a slight hope— maybe the Emperor would pardon him. With the pass of time he became more and more desperate. What could he do? According to the laws of the Han Dynasty, he could use money to redeem himself, but he did not have money. If there had been anyone who could lend him a helping hand, who would say a few words on his behalf to the Emperor, he would have his punishment greatly reduced. However, most of the people just wanted to be distanced from him as faraway as possible. The philosophy of "minding your own businesses" had made people cold and relentless. In the time of the Han Dynasty, many ministers, when condemned by the emperor and were ordered an investigation, they would commit suicide to retain their nobility. Sima Qian thought about his own status. What was he? He had to face the cruel reality that he was only a historian who was in charge of literature, history, astrology and the calendar. He was not very different from those sorcerers who were in charge of divination. He was only a servant of the Emperor's interests. In the eyes of the emperor, he was like the actors and performers dancing and singing on the stage. He certainly belonged to those who were being looked down on by society. After this blow, Sima Qian realised his state of slavery. Emperor Wu had a group of literati around him, for example, the productive Yan Zhu, who "claimed to be like the actors" ; funny, clever yet grumpy Dongfang Shuo, who wrote "On Questions Put Forth" and "On Mr. Fei You" and also Sima Xiangru, who was Emperor Wu's favourite but often didn't come to court, claiming that he was ill. These people did not enjoy the environment they were in but they had no way of getting out of it. Sima Qian, just like them, was merely a toy in the Emperor's hands, doing something related to culture and entertainment. The Emperor would execute a Grand Scribe like killing an ant.

Sima Qian thought that he was not born into a noble family, and yet if he were to die wrongly accused, it would be extremely unfair. The accusation was

月光射进囚室，一个黑须黑发四十多岁的囚徒，便遍身沐浴在惨白色的光波之中了。他一动不动地跪坐在草荐上，像一尊铁的塑像。他炯炯的目光凝视着暗处，仿佛那里隐藏着什么害人的怪物。

司马迁入狱之后，手脚戴上了刑具，整天提心吊胆，被狱吏敲扑，受狱卒斥骂。种种凌辱，使他多次想到自杀。但他还抱有一线希望——皇帝或许会谅解的吧！随着时光的流逝，他越来越绝望了！怎么办呢？汉朝有用金钱赎罪的规定，可是他没有钱！如果能有朋友救助，如果皇帝左右的亲近哪怕能给讲一句话，罪责也能减轻许多。可是，势利的人们见他遭了殃都躲得远远的，"明哲保身"的哲学使人们变得冷漠无情了。汉朝有不少公卿大臣，当皇帝降罪，必须接受审问时，便立即自杀，以保持高贵的身份。可是自己又是怎样的身份呢？这时，他才痛切地感到：从事文学、历史、天文、历法这些文化工作的史臣，也就和管求神问卦的卜、祝差不多，是供皇帝玩耍消遣的，在皇帝眼中也就和弄歌舞杂耍的倡优一样。因此也是被社会上一般人看不起的。经过这一巨大打击，司马迁才痛切地感受到自己为奴隶的命运！汉武帝周围聚集着一批文学侍从之臣，像作赋多篇却"自悔类倡"的严助，滑稽多智而又写作了《答客难》和《非有先生论》大发牢骚的东方朔，辞赋最为武帝欣赏却常称病不朝的司马相如，这些人都不满意所处的地位，但又无从摆脱。司马迁也和他们一样，虽然自己很重视史官的职责，可是在武帝眼里，一切文化工作不过是点缀升平，娱乐心意的玩意儿。他处死一个太史令也就跟捏死一只蚂蚁差不多！

司马迁想到，本来没有什么高贵的身份，背着冤屈的罪名白白地死去，太不值得了。罪名！对，是"诬上"之罪，为什

"blaspheming the Emperor." How could he have blasphemed the emperor by saying a few lines about justice? The penalty for such a crime was death. There were more ridiculous crimes, such as "silent protest." (Yan Yi, the Grand Minister of Agriculture, merely moved his lips and was accused by Zhang Tang of protesting and Yan was executed.) Silent protest! What a crime! When thinking about this, a sneer appeared on Sima Qian's angry face. "No, I must not die now." "Death may be as weighty as Mount Tai, or it may be as insignificant as a goose feather." To die now would be to die as light as a goose feather.

Sima Qian thought about the great figures in history who had struggled in times of hardship. Xibo, the King (Wen) of the Zhou Dynasty was imprisoned and he analysed *The Book of Changes*; Confucius was in distress and he created *The Spring and Autumn Annals (Chunqiu)*; Qu Yuan was banished and he composed his poem "The Lament." Sima Qian stood up and walked about in excitement. "I must learn from their examples. I must learn from them. I must turn my sorrow and anger into words."

But, in order to live, he would have to accept castration. What kind of shame would that be! Sima Qian could see the humiliating eyes, like arrows in his chest. He could hear abusive words pouring over him like water. "No, No! I cannot take this." He was in extreme pain. He raised his hands and asked, "Heaven, what should I do? What should I do?"

The moon had already set to the west and daylight had come. After thorough consideration, Sima Qian made his final decision: he wanted to write *Records of the Grand Historian*, a history book that would make him immortal, a book "to examine all that concerns Heaven and man, to illustrate the changes of the past and present, and complete a work of my own." He was determined: I have been deprived of everything, but I still have a pen. I will record the great images of the brave generals and loyal ministers. I will expose the true nature of the evil people, too, so that people in the future can learn from these examples. I will use my pen to record the changes of the past 3, 000 years, and to record all the unfair things on earth!

Du Zhou, the new Grandee Secretary, upon hearing Sima Qian's decision to accept castration, was dumbfounded. He had thought Sima Qian would stick to his guns. If Sima Qian did so, Du Zhou would have a chance to demonstrate his power and abilities. It was out of expectations that Sima Qian made such a decision. "This dumb book worm," Du Zhou thought, "he is also afraid of death."

么替李陵讲了几句公道话就是"诬上"呢？这可是死罪啊！不过，无独有偶，不是还有"腹诽"罪吗（有人对大司农颜异议论法令不便，颜异没开口，只把嘴唇翘了翘，张汤便说他心怀不满，以"腹诽"判了他死罪）。那又是什么样的罪过！想到这里，司马迁悲愤的脸上竟也挂上了一丝冷笑。不，决不能死！"死有重于泰山，或轻于鸿毛"，白白地去死，不是比鸿毛还轻么！

于是，古代的志士仁人，在困苦中发奋，在挫折中振起的种种光辉形象，纷至沓来地呈现在他的眼前了："西伯（周文王）拘而演《周易》；仲尼（孔子）厄而作《春秋》；屈原放逐，乃赋《离骚》……"他站了起来，激动地走着，应该效法他们！应该效法他们！把一腔悲愤托之于文字吧！

可是！要想保留生命，必须接受宫刑！那又是怎样的奇耻大辱！那讥嘲的眼光，将像支支利箭，时时穿透你的心胸；那侮辱性的话语，将像污泥浊水向你劈头盖脸地泼来。不，不能接受，宁死也不能接受！可是……他痛苦极了，举手问天：天啊！我该何所抉择，何所抉择啊！

月亮已经向西倾斜，天快亮了。司马迁经过反复地苦思，终于作出了他的抉择：一定要完成不朽的事业，写完这一部"究天人之际，通古今之变，成一家之言"的《史记》。一切都被剥夺了，但我还有一支笔，这支笔要树立忠臣义士的形象，要照出魑魅魍魉的原形，为后代作鉴戒；这支笔要描绘出三千年的风云变幻，尽写出人间的不平！

当新提升的御史大夫杜周，听到司马迁愿受宫刑的消息时，简直目瞪口呆了。他原以为司马迁不会屈服，那么，他正可以大显身手一番。谁料想司马迁竟选择了这条路。他想：这些讲究气节的书呆子，原来也是贪生怕死的。

However, Emperor Wu was very happy when he heard of Sima Qian's choice. He thought: no matter how rebellious the horse was, it would succumb to my power. The Grand Scribe also had his back broken under me. After the torture, Sima Qian was appointed Prefect of Writing to the Palace. This was a very important position at court, overseeing documents of a confidential nature. After all, Emperor Wu appreciated Sima Qian's literary achievements.

After being appointed to the position, Sima Qian still thought about the humiliation he had suffered. Sometimes he "felt lost inside the house and sometimes he would have no idea where to go after leaving his front door." The only thing that kept him living on was writing. He kept writing, day and night. After the incident and the torture, he had gained a better understanding of society.

What best described Sima Qian's feelings at that time was a letter he wrote in response to his friend, Ren An. This letter was collected in *The Chronicles of the Han Dynasty (Hanshu)* — *The Biography of Sima Qian* and named "Letter to Ren An." This is a letter describing all the wrongs that he had suffered. It is also the most direct and genuine material for researching the character of Sima Qian. After becoming the Prefect of Writing to the Palace, Sima Qian received a letter from his friend Ren An, the Regional Inspector at Yizhou. In the letter, Ren An criticised his friend for not following the good examples of the ancient sages by carefully choosing friends, and recommending good people to the imperial court. Ren An, at that time, did not know of Sima Qian's situation. How could Sima Qian respond to such a letter? And, he delayed as long as possible.

In the later years of Emperor Wu's reign, poverty drove people to rebellious action. The capital city of Chang'an was not peaceful either. In the winter of the 1st year of the Zhenghe Period, a large scale raid even took place in Shanglin, the imperial hunting ground. The city gates were closed for 11 days. Not only had the social crisis become widespread, the internal conflicts inside the imperial courts had also escalated. Some claimed that the family of Gongsun He, who was the Prime Minister and relative of the Empress, and Princess Yangshi, along with Princess Zhuyi, took part in witchcraft to curse the Emperor. They planted voodoo dolls under the main roads. This witchcraft scandal resulted in the execution of imperial relatives, princesses and many others. When the Emperor was old, he became very suspicious. When he fell ill, he listened to his close minister Jiang Chong's words that witchcraft was being planned to curse him. A large scale search was conducted in the capital city of Chang'an. With Jiang Chong's abuse of power, tens of thousands of

汉武帝知道司马迁愿受宫刑却十分高兴：什么样的骏马也得听我驾驭，这小小的太史令的傲骨终于被折断了。司马迁从蚕室里出来之后，武帝便任命他为中书令。中书令职掌诏诰答表等机密事情，是皇帝宫廷里的要职，武帝对他的文才毕竟是很欣赏的。

司马迁担任中书令以后，耻辱感时时缠绕着他，使他经常处于精神恍惚的状态，在家坐着便好像丢失了什么，出门则不知道该到哪里去。所谓"居则忽忽若有所亡，出则不知所如往"。支持他活下去的唯一的事情便是写作。他夜以继日地撰述着，修改着。经过这番挫折，他对所处社会的认识大大提高了。

最能反映司马迁受刑之后心情的，是他写给友人任安的一封复信。这封信收录在《汉书·司马迁传》中，后来被称作《报任安书》。这是一篇血泪文字，也是研究司马迁生平最真实、最直接的资料。司马迁任中书令数年之后，友人益州刺史任安给他写了一封信，批评他没有像古代贤臣那样，谨慎择友，向朝廷推举贤才。任安太不了解他的处境，更不了解他的心情，如何能够解释清楚呢？司马迁迟迟没有下笔。

汉武帝晚年，弄到民穷财尽，许多地方发生动乱。长安城中也很不安定，征和元年冬，甚至闹到大规模搜查上林苑，关闭城门十一天。不仅社会危机严重，皇帝家族的内讧也愈演愈烈。有人上告皇后的亲戚丞相公孙贺家和皇帝的妹妹阳石公主以及诸邑公主利用巫祝诅咒皇帝，并在大道上埋木偶人搞巫术暗害。这些活动被称为"巫蛊"。追究结果皇亲公主一大批被杀。武帝晚年多疑，生了病，近臣江充便说皇帝生病是因为有人搞巫蛊暗害，于是大肆搜查，江充栽赃陷害，城中冤杀了几万人。江充与太子有矛盾，怕太子接位对他不利，于是乘机说

people were killed. Jiang Chong, who had grudges against with the heir apparent, was afraid that, after the heir apparent became the Emperor, he would be punished. Jiang Chong then created rumours that there was witchcraft afoot in the imperial courts. He then obtained orders to carry out a thorough search of the imperial courts. He had set a lot of people up. In the end, he claimed that he had found voodoo dolls in the court of the heir apparent, who could not explain away and killed Jiang Chong. The heir apparent took up arms and was being chased by Liu Qumao, an ally of the King of Changyi who opposed the heir apparent. The heir apparent fled and later committed suicide. The Empress and other ministers who were related all committed suicide. This case was rectified within one year. Emperor Wu punished those ministers who had turned against the heir apparent at the time, and executed Liu Qumao and others. General Li Guangli, a relative of the King of Changyi, surrendered to the Xiongnu because of the suppression that happened in the 3rd year of the Zhenghe Period (90 B.C.). Ren An was implicated as well. When the heir apparent took up arms, Ren An received his orders to send out troops. Because Ren An wanted to wait and find out more about the situation, he did not support the heir apparent. He was later charged and thrown into jail. Judging the situation, Sima Qian thought if he did not respond to Ren An's letter, he would never get the chance again. In his letter, Sima Qian wrote frankly, in reply to a friend who was going to die. He would not hold anything back. He wanted his friend to understand him. Sima Qian also said that even though he was still alive he yet felt as if he had died. He said this in support of his friend. Not long after the letter, Ren An was cut in half at the waist.

How did Sima Qian's life end? There is no record in the historical books and opinions differ among researchers. One theory is that Sima Qian was killed, and it was based on *The Commentaries on Old Rites in the Chronicles of the Han Dynasty* written by Wei Hong of the Eastern Han Dynasty. The book itself is now not available but the record was kept in *Collected Annotations of the* Shiji compiled by Pei Yin.

According to Wei Hong, Sima Qian commented on Emperor Jing's errors in "The Annals of Emperor Jing." Upon reading that his father was being criticised, Emperor Wu was furious and deleted the chapter. Later Emperor Wu threw Sima Qian into the Silk Worm Chamber (Castration Chamber) where Sima Qian "complained" and then he was thrown into prison and died there. There are many problems with Wei Hong's description. In "The Postface to the Shiji" and also in "The Letter to Ren An," Sima Qian mentioned that he was imprisoned and was then being put into the Silk Worm Chamber, contrary to

宫中也有蛊气。他奉命在宫中大搜查，制造了不少冤案，最后一直查到皇后和太子，说是在太子宫中挖出了桐木人，太子无法自辩，于是杀江充，起兵反抗。丞相刘屈牦是与太子争位的昌邑王一党，发兵攻打太子，太子逃亡，随即自杀，皇后与受牵连的大臣都自杀，这个大冤案一年之后就得到平反。汉武帝反过来惩治当时不支持太子、镇压太子的大臣们的罪，于是刘屈牦等被杀，昌邑王的亲戚、领兵在外的贰师将军李广利则索性投降了匈奴。这件事发生在征和三年（公元前90年）。其时任安也受到了牵连。太子发兵时，他本已接受了太子发兵的命令，后来意存观望，又不支持太子，追究起来就被逮捕入狱，当时的情势恐怕是难免一死的。司马迁想到，如果再不复信就永远没有复信的机会了。所以在复信中他坦率地说：如果您忽然逝去，我将永远不能将我愤懑不平的心情向您倾诉，您的灵魂，也会始终感到遗憾！给将死的友人复信，他再没有什么顾虑，他希望友人能理解他，同时诉说自己虽生犹死的心情，也是对友人的一份支持与安慰吧！果然，没有多久，任安被腰斩。

司马迁的结局如何呢？史书上没有明确记载，研究者意见也较为分歧。一种意见认为司马迁是被杀害的，其主要根据是东汉卫宏《汉书旧仪注》上的记载。此书已散佚，这段记载保存在裴的《史记集解》里。

卫宏说司马迁写《景帝本纪》，讲了汉景帝的缺点过失。汉武帝大怒，将《景帝本纪》删除了，后来因李陵的事，将他下了蚕室，有怨言，关进监狱而死。这段话漏洞颇多，比如司马迁的《自序》和《报任安书》这两篇文章都讲先下狱然后才决定接受宫刑下蚕室，而不是如卫宏所说先下蚕室后下狱。接受宫刑后，司马迁确实做了若干时日的中书令，《报任安书》

what Wei Hong had said. After the castration, Sima Qian did become the Prefect of Writing to the Palace for a while, as was shown in "The Letter to Ren An." The reason Sima Qian succumbed to castration was that he wanted to finish the compilation of the *Shiji*. If he had not done that, it would not have been possible for Emperor Wu to have read "The Annals of Emperor Jing" and "The Annals of the Current Emperor," and would not have been able to "carve it off and throw it away." If Sima Qian had died then, he would not have completed the *Shiji*. However, according to "The Letter to Ren An," Sima Qian clearly stated that the *Shiji* has "130 chapters" and "I have actually compiled this book." Besides, Sima Qian compiled the *Shiji* not at the order of the Emperor, and Emperor Wu may not have seen the book. According to *The Chronicles of the Han Dynasty—The Biography of Sima Qian*, the *Shiji* was disclosed after Sima Qian's death. It was Sima Qian's maternal grandson Yang Yun who released the *Shiji* during the reign of Emperor Xuan. If Sima Qian's "complaint" was a reference to "The Letter to Ren An," then this letter full of complaints could have led to the death penalty. The general consensus among many researchers is that Sima Qian died at the age of 60, in the last years of Emperor Wu's reign, or in the early years of Emperor Zhao's reign. However the exact year and circumstance of his death cannot be determined.

Apart from the *Shiji*, did Sima Qian write any other books? *The Chronicles of the Han Dynasty—Logs of Artistic Books* has listed "eight odes by Sima Qian" ; *The Chronicles of the Sui Dynasty—The Collections of Ancient Books* compiled in the early years of Tang Dynasty has "one chapter of work by Sima Qian, the Prefect of Writing to the Palace of the Han," however the book has been lost. Only three articles are currently extant. They are "The Letter to Ren An," "Ode of the Literati," and "The Letter to Dear Bo Ling." "The Letter to Ren An" has already been mentioned. "Ode of the Literati" was an article mentioned by Tao Qian and Liu Xiaobiao in the times after Sima Qian. This Ode may be the work of Sima Qian. The last article, "The Letter to Dear Bo Ling" was believed to be someone else's work and was mistakenly put under Sima Qian's name. Besides all these three, there are two other chapters from the Liang Dynasty, titled "Exellent Comments by King Su." They are obviously others' work using Sima Qian's name, and they have been lost, too. It is fair to say that apart from the *Shiji*, "The Letter to Ren An" is the most important work by Sima Qian.

Sima Qian died without having had many children. According to reliable records he had one daughter, who married Yang Chang, who was once Prime Minister during Emperor Zhao's reign. She was very knowledgeable and

有明确的记载，而不是下蚕室和死接踵而至。司马迁忍耻受宫刑，是为了完成《史记》这部著作，在这之前武帝也不大可能得见《景帝本纪》和《今上本纪》，也不可能"削而投之"，因为那样一来，司马迁修订《史记》的工作便无从进行了。在《报任安书》中，已明确讲到《史记》"凡百三十篇""仆诚已著此书"，可见此时《史记》已完成。再说《史记》并非奉旨撰写，汉武帝可能根本未见过。照《汉书·司马迁传》的说法，司马迁死后，《史记》才稍有出现，直到汉宣帝时，司马迁的外孙杨恽才正式对外宣布。不过，如果说"有怨言"指的是《报任安书》这篇充满怨愤的文章，那么由此招来横祸以至"下狱死"，倒是很有可能的。为多数研究者认可的通常的说法是司马迁死于汉武帝末年，或汉昭帝初年，约六十岁，具体的年代以及死因都无可考证了。

《史记》之外，司马迁还有没有别的作品呢？《汉书·艺文志》曾著录"司马迁赋八篇"，唐初修撰的《隋书·经籍志》也著录有"汉中书令司马迁集一卷"系后人所辑，后来也散佚了。现在还留存的有《报任安书》、《悲士不遇赋》和《与挚伯陵书》等三篇文章。《报任安书》已如前述，《悲士不遇赋》，陶潜、刘孝标都曾提到，可能确是司马迁所作。《与挚伯陵书》，一般都怀疑是别人的作品，误挂在司马迁名下。此外梁代还有《太史公素王妙议》二卷，显系伪托，并且已亡佚。可以说，司马迁的著作，除《史记》外，只有《报任安书》最重要。

司马迁身后也很萧条，他的后代可以考知的是有一个女儿，这个女儿嫁给了汉昭帝时做过丞相的杨敞。她很有见识，很有魄力，对杨敞帮助很大。司马迁的外孙杨恽因消灭霍氏谋反集

decisive. She provided great assistance to her husband Yang Chang. Yang Yun, son of Yang Chang became Marquis of Pingtong because of his crackdown on rebellious moves in the House of Huo. Yang Yun, however, commented on current issues and people, and was banished. Then he became very grumpy and wrote a famous article, "The Letter to Sun Huizong." This article, similar in style to "The Letter to Ren An," also criticised the current situation, but was not as touching. Because of this letter and other crimes, Yang Yun was cut into two at the waist, suffering a similar fate to that of his grandfather. The reason that Yang Yun could disclose the *Shiji* was firstly that he had the title of Marquis of Ping Tong, and secondly, he was living in the times of Emperor Xuan. This emperor, Liu Xun, was Emperor Wu's great grandson. Liu Xun's grandparents and parents were killed because of the witchcraft scandals. He was just an infant when he was thrown into prison. Fortunately he was able to survive because of a jailer who allowed a female prisoner to breastfeed him. Because of all this, Liu Xun would not have liked his great grandfather. He would, therefore, not mind if the history books described the errors of his great grandfather. Apart from one daughter, it is hard to determine whether Sima Qian had any other children. He had a lonely life and could be childless but the *Shiji* serves as a monument that will last forever.

团有功，被封为平通侯。但他也喜欢议论时事，讥评人物，因此遭到贬谪。被贬谪后他牢骚满腹，写了一篇著名的《报孙会宗书》。这篇文章基调与《报任安书》相同，讽刺牢骚则有过之，但深刻感人却远远不及。由于这封信和其他罪状，杨恽竟被腰斩，可说是继承了他外祖父的不幸的命运。杨恽所以能公布《史记》，一是因为他有平通侯的爵位，二是因为他处在汉宣帝时代。宣帝刘询是武帝的曾孙，他的祖父母、父母都因巫蛊之祸被害。他当时还是个婴儿，也被投入狱中，多亏一位狱吏保护，并让女囚用乳水喂养他，好不容易才活了下来。怎么说，他对他的曾祖父都不会有多少好感。史臣记载他曾祖父的过失，他大概不会去追究的。除女儿外，司马迁是否还有别的后代，就不得而知了。他身后寂寞，但一部《史记》却为他树立了永久的丰碑！

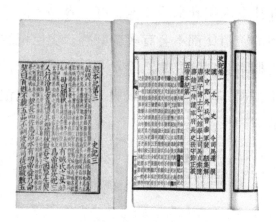

《史记》书影

Photocopies of *Shiji*

I A General History of 3,000 Years

Sima Qian had planned to write a general history starting in ancient times and ending in his own times. Where should he start? According to *The Book of History* (*Shangshu*), Yao and Shun were the earliest records. The histories of the Yellow Emperor contained many mystic legends, which were by the scholars to be unreliable. However, Sima Qian, after being to Kongtong, Zhuolu and places near the coasts and the Yangtse River and Huai River, had learnt many stories from the locals there about the Yellow Emperor, Yao and Shun. He also felt that the customs preserved there were different from those in other places. Sima Qian checked records in *The Spring and Autumn Annals*, and also in *The History of Different States* (*Guoyu*) and discovered that records of the Yellow Emperor and others were not simply fabrications. He realised that some ancient books may have been lost, and that he should not rely purely on existing books to decide the starting point of the general history. After some thoughts, Sima Qian decided to start writing his book with the Yellow Emperor. The Yellow Emperor of the Xuanyuan clan was actually a tribal leader living in the late Neolithic Age. He represented a historical phase in the development of the peoples of China. Because his clan, along with another important clan, that of the Yan Emperor, became one of the most important clans among the Chinese peoples. The Chinese, for a very long time, had called themselves the descendants of the Yan (and) Huang (of Yan Emperor and Yellow Emperor). The *Shiji*, the first general history ever compiled, starts its records with the Yellow Emperor. Basing his work on legends passed down, Sima Qian chose the most reasonable and sensible records and determined that the Yellow Emperor was the ancestor of the Chinese peoples. There was another reason for Sima Qian to start his narrative with the Yellow Emperor. Many traditions and customs and some systems and agricultural techniques had been passed down by the Yellow Emperor and he was considered the model for all. This role-model had inspired many people. One of them was Lu Xun, the known writer in modern Chinese history, who wrote, "I would shed my blood for Xuanyuan." Lu Xun used Xuanyuan as the alias for China and the Chinese peoples. He also expressed his passion for his country and his determination that he would devote his life to it.

How to compile a history covering 3,000 years was Sima Qian's next problem. If he were to follow the examples of *The Spring and Autumn Annals,* or *The Annals Compiled by Zuo* (*Zuozhuan*), both of which used chronological order to record historical events, Sima Qian's annals would record events year

（一） 三千年的通史

司马迁计划写一部从古代直至当时的通史。从哪儿写起呢？文字记载，《尚书》从尧舜开始算最早的了。传说中的黄帝等等则夹杂了许多奇异的神话，以至大人先生们觉得难以称道。然而，司马迁到过崆峒、涿鹿，还到过海边和江淮一带，听到长老们讲述黄帝、尧、舜的遗迹，觉得那里的风俗都不同一般。他又查考了《春秋》、《国语》中的记载，更相信黄帝等等并非子虚乌有。古书早有缺佚，因此不应全凭书本来决定这部通史的起点。经过这样一番考虑，《史记》便从黄帝写起。其实黄帝轩辕氏大约是新石器晚期一个部落联盟的领袖。他代表了我们民族发展的一个历史阶段。因为黄帝族是后来繁衍为中华民族的最主要的一支，故而从古代起，我们民族便称作黄帝子孙（或再加上另外重要的一支炎帝族而称为炎黄子孙）。《史记》作为第一部通史著作，从关于黄帝的大量神话传说中，选择其中比较合乎情理的记载下来，确认黄帝是我们民族的祖先。从黄帝开始还有一个作用，古史传说一些合理的制度、风习，一些有用的制作，都是从黄帝开始的，可以作为后世的榜样。《史记》从黄帝开始，对后世是产生了巨大影响的。鲁迅著名的诗句："我以我血荐轩辕"，就是以轩辕氏为祖国、民族的代称，要将自己的一腔热血奉献给他，从而抒发了强烈的热爱祖国的情怀。

从黄帝轩辕氏直到当时的汉武帝，这一部三千年的历史如何编法，是司马迁须要考虑的第二个问题。按《春秋》、《左传》的办法，逐年记载，即"编年体"吧，历史事件发生的次序

by year, which was a good way to render the sequence of events. However, records of the characters in the events would be scattered into different years and chapters, and also be interrupted by records of other characters. This would make it hard to achieve a coherent record of characters. If Sima Qian were to write pure biographies, even though he could have put the major stories of the characters together and given detailed accounts of them, it would have been hard to touch upon major events that had happened during those years. It would have been even harder to record other major economical and cultural events of the time in the biography of one person. In order to solve this problem, Sima Qian used his creativity and initiated a biographical style of history keeping. There are five major categories in the *Shiji*.

1. The twelve chapters of Annals. These annals are imperial biographies of the emperors, describing the major political events of each dynasty. "The Annals of the Five Emperors" was followed by "The Annals of the Xia," "Annals of the Yin" and "Annals of the Zhou." The Qin Dynasty was recorded in two parts, in "The Annals of the Feudal State of Qin" and also "The Annals of the First Emperor of the Qin." These two annals could have been put together, along the lines of the previous three annals; however, because of the importance of the First Emperor of the Qin's unification of China, and the lengthy record of the details, Sima Qian used two chapters for the Qin. The first chapter started before the founding of the Qin Dynasty. The second chapter dealt with events from the times of Xiang Yu all the way to Emperor Wu of the Han Dynasty. Major events in the "reigns" of each of the top leaders were recorded in detail. Even though Xiang Yu and Empress Lü did not actually become emperors, they did hold ultimate power to issue decrees, and so Sima Qian categorised them as emperors. The Annals of Empress Lü was recorded instead of the annals of the emperor of the time, Emperor Hui of the Han. This revealed Sima Qian's spirit of pursuing the truth. It is also true and clear that Sima Qian spent more time describing current and recent affairs than ancient stories.

2. The twelve chronological Tables. Sima Qian used chronological tables to clearly display a record of historical events. The first table is "The Genealogical Table of the Three Ages," which recorded the history of the legendary five emperors to the three dynasties of Xia, Shang and Zhou (840 B.C, the first year of Gonghe Period, the year when China started to have accurate yearly records). It is very hard to verify the records of ancient histories. However, scripts of oracle bones unearthed in archaeological excavations in Yin Dynasty revealed similar records that were described in the *Shiji*. This demonstrates the accuracy of Sima Qian's work. Even though records of

是清楚了，但是，一个历史人物的事迹却不免被分散到好多年中，而且被别的人、事隔断，不能给读者以鲜明的印象。如果全用人物传记，历史人物的事迹集中，面貌比较清晰，可是逐年发生的大事，未必都能涉及，而经济、文化的发展变化则更难容纳在内。为解决这种种困难，司马迁充分地发挥了他的首创精神，确立了"纪传体"这一种体裁。"纪传体"的《史记》，包括五部分：

1. "本纪"十二篇。以各代帝王为中心，叙述每一个朝代的兴衰和重要的政治事件。在记黄帝等的《五帝本纪》之后，即接以《夏本纪》、《殷本纪》、《周本纪》，记夏、商、周三个朝代的兴亡大事。秦代是分成了《秦本纪》和《秦始皇本纪》两篇，照夏、殷、周本纪的写法，原可合为一篇的，但因为秦始皇统一天下的作用至为重要，篇幅也较长，故而分成了两篇。《秦本纪》是秦国发展史，叙述到始皇之前。《秦始皇本纪》以下从项羽起直到汉武帝，每一代最高统治者的生平大事都有较详细的记录。其中项羽、吕后虽没有皇帝的名义，但一个时期他们是政令的发布人，《史记》也就将之列为本纪，以吕后代替名义上的皇帝——汉惠帝。这是司马迁求实精神的表现。从《本纪》的分量看，司马迁是详今略古的。

2. "表"十篇。为使历史大事一目了然，《史记》采用了表格形式。首先是《三代世表》，从传说中的五帝以至夏、商、周（一直到共和元年——公元前840年，我国开始有确切纪年）时代，列为简表。古史渺茫，本难考信，可是殷墟甲骨文所记殷代世系，竟与《史记》所载基本相同。这告诉我们，司马迁

ancient times may not be trusted fully, we cannot disregard them lightly. "The Chronological Table of the Feudal Lords" comes next. This table records the history of twelve major feudal states (thirteen, if the State of Wu, which became a strong power, is also included). The history starts from the Gonghe Period and finishes in the Spring and Autumn Period. "The Yearly Chronicle of the Six States" is the next. This table records the history of the Warring States Period when the seven strong states fought. It covers the major events over 270 years, from the end of the Spring and Autumn Period to the second emperor of the Qin Dynasty. After this table comes "The Monthly Table of the Events Between Qin and Chu." From the time Chen She first rose in arms to the time of Liu Bang's enthronement as the First Emperor of the Han, there were rapid changes in the situation and Sima Qian recorded events each month. The following two tables, "The Chronological Table of the Lords of the Han Clan" and "The Chronological Table of the Officials Who Became Marquises in the Time of Emperor Gaozu of the Han," describe the situation of enfeoffment of all feudal kings, and the changes and activities of famous generals and ministers.

3. The eight Treatises. The eight treatises include commentaries and discourses which are like a specific history of culture and the systems. The eight treatises are as follows. ① "The Treatise on Rites," which describes events and rituals. Early versions were missing and "On Rites Written by Xunzi" was inserted in the *Shiji*. Sima Qian emphasised that the setting up of rituals should take into consideration the people so that it could serve the political needs of the emperors. ② "The Treatise on Music," which comments on the affairs of music. Some chapters were also lost. People late complemented it by inserting into the *Shiji* a chapter of "The Rite and Music." According to Sima Qian, music could be used for the betterment of society. Music could touch people's heart and influence social culture. This is the theme of "The Rite and Music." ③ "The Treatise on Bells (Harmony and Measurement)" mainly discusses military affairs. Sima Qian considered the six notes of the music to be the foundation of all things, especially of military law. His view on military was that "without military force, [a nation] would not become strong; without virtue to touch and change people, [it would] not become prosperous." This is why military books were also called books of music. In "Bells" the text from the discussion of music showcases the importance attached to music in ancient China, and also demonstrates the outstanding achievements China has had in music. A set of chime bells, the Zenghouyi Chime Bells, unearthed in 1978 in Sui County in Hubei Province, was proved to be the earliest super large-sized fixed-tune instrument that operated on a twelve and a half tonal range (from C2

撰表，确有根据，《史记》所载远古历史固不可全信，然而也不应轻易地加以否定。紧接《三代世表》之后，是《十二诸侯年表》。这表从共和始至春秋结束，将十二个主要诸侯国（连后来称霸的吴则有十三国）的纪年大事列表对照。其后则为《六国表》，大致是表列春秋后从周元王元年直至秦二世共二百七十年这一时期的历史大事，主要是记载战国时代七雄纷争的史事。《六国表》后，即为《秦楚之际月表》，从陈涉起义到汉高祖刘邦称帝，这期间斗争形势瞬息万变，故而编成月表，保留较详细的记录。这以下《汉兴以来诸侯年表》、《高祖功臣侯年表》等，都是汉王朝建立以后分封诸侯的情况，以及将相名臣的活动、更换情况。

3. "书"八篇。"八书"有论有述，类似文化、制度专史。这八篇包括：①《礼书》，论述礼仪之类的事。早已有亡缺，后人以《荀子·礼论》等篇补入。司马迁论"礼"强调近性情通王道。认为礼仪的设定，应符合人情人性，为王道政治服务。②《乐书》，论述音乐方面的事。《乐书》也有缺失，后人以《礼记·乐记》补充。照司马迁的观点，音乐是用来移风易俗的。音乐能感动人，从而影响社会风气。这也是《乐记》的观点。③《律书》，正文主要讲兵事。因作者认为六律是万事的根本，对于军事尤其重要。作者的军事观，主要是："非兵不强，非德不昌。"就是说为抵御侵略，没有军队是不行的，但是只靠武力而不以德感化，那也昌盛不了。故论兵事而称律书。又《律书》于"太史公曰"以下即详论音律，反映了我国古代

to D7). It demonstrated that China had long been using heptachord scales. Transposition could also be achieved on the Chime Bells. The unearthing of the relics could be used as a supplement to the records of the *Shiji*, which also recorded the splendid achievements of China's musical history. ④ "The Treatise on Calendars" describes the law of calendars. It discussed the interchanging and transformation between the six tunes and six rhythms and the Lunar and Solar of calendars. It also introduced the five calendars from the times of Emperor Zhuanxu. The "Calendars" finally introduced in details the changing of Taichu (Grand Inception) Calendar to Yuan Calendar that was considered to be the most comprehensive calendar. ⑤ "The Treatise on Astronomy" describes and records the natural astrological phenomena. On the one hand, it criticises the unreliability of overreliance on astrological divination; on the other hand, it quotes from ancient records to demonstrate the existence of a link between astrological signs and human events. ⑥ "The Treatise on the *Fengshan* Ceremony." *Fengshan* Ceremony is a grand ceremony for emperors to make sacrifices to the heavens and the earth, the mountains and rivers after they achieved the unification of a country. Apart from the detailed description of ceremony, "The Treatise on the *Fengshan* Ceremony" also discloses Emperor Wu's superstitious pursuit of immortality. ⑦ "The Treatise on Rivers and Canals" sings highly of the achievements of Yu the Great for his hydraulic projects to control the floods and continues to discuss the hydraulic projects in the years after and experiences and lessons learnt. It also provides a detailed record of Emperor Wu's control-flood actions in the Huzi River. ⑧ "The Treatise on Equalization" discusses the economic recovery in the early years of the Han Dynasty. Emperor Wu, based on the economic strength, built a strong country. However, the development created many defects in the areas of politics, economy and the military, and caused serious social and political problems. The eight chapters have very important value for research on the history of science, culture and economy in ancient China.

4. Thirty chapters of Feudal Houses. These chapters record the history of feudal houses in the Spring and Autumn Period, a brief history of the Marquis of the Liu family and the empresses, and also brief biographies of important ministers of the Han Dynasty, for example, Xiao He, Cao Can, Zhang Liang, Chen Ping and Zhou Bo. Besides, there are two special chapters: "The House of Confucius" and "The House of Chen She." Even though Confucius was not a Marquis, due to his great contribution to the culture and academy he was treated as a feudal house. Chen She, a leader of the rebellious farmers, took up arms at the end of the Qin Dynasty. He declared himself king. Because he was

对音律的重视和辉煌的成果。1978年我国湖北随县出土的曾侯乙墓编钟，经研究测定，是目前世界上已知最早的具有十二半音阶关系的特大型定调乐器，它证明我国早就运用七声音阶，而且还能旋宫转调。对出土文物的研究，可以补充《史记》之不足，但《史记》毕竟记录了我国古代音乐文化高度发展的史实。④《历书》，讲历法。论述六律六吕与历法的阴阳交替变化，介绍了颛顼以来的五种历法，最后详细介绍太初改元，认为是最完备的历法。⑤《天官书》，讲星象。客观地记录天象。一方面批评过度讲星象预示吉凶的不合常理，另一方面却也举出古书所记，认为天象与人事确有某种感应存在。⑥《封禅书》。封禅是完成统一大业的帝王祭祀天地山川，报告成功的大典礼。《封禅书》除记载各种祭祀典礼外，对汉武帝迷信神仙企求长生的活动，多有揭露。⑦《河渠书》，一开始即盛赞大禹治水的功绩，然后讲后世的水利建设以及治水的经验教训，对于汉武帝塞瓠子的活动则有较详记载。⑧《平准书》，论述了汉初的经济恢复，以及汉武帝凭藉强大的经济力量，达到了空前的强盛。但在政治、经济、军事上都有很多弊端，出现了许多严重的社会政治问题。以上"八书"对于科学史、文化史、经济史的研究都有着十分重要的价值。

4."世家"三十篇。主要记述春秋战国各诸侯国的历史，汉代刘姓诸侯王和汉朝皇后的简史，以及汉朝开国功臣——萧何、曹参、张良、陈平、周勃的小传。除此之外，尚有《孔子世家》、《陈涉世家》二篇。孔子虽不是王侯，但因其对于学术文化贡献特大，故被列为世家。陈涉是秦末农民起义领袖，自称为王，

the first to rebel with force and the nobles, kings, generals, and officials he sent out succeeded in overthrowing the Qin. Hence, Sima Qian broke with tradition and included Chen She in the thirty Houses.

5. Seventy chapters of the Biographies. It is the collection of biographies of people dating back from the former Qin Dynasty to Sima Qian's times, including people from all walks of life, such as nobles, generals, politicians, military figures, literati, economists, hermits, assassins, harsh officials, gallant wandering Knights, fortune-tellers and merchants. Apart from these, some other chapters, such as "The Biographies of the Xiongnu" and "The Biographies of the Dawan," describe the history of ethnic minority groups and the neighbouring countries. "The Postface to the *Shiji*" is the last chapter of the Biographies, with a summary of each chapter. In the end of the Postface, it indicates there are 130 chapters in the *Shiji*, with 526,500 characters and five sections in total.

According to research, these five categories of writings were not invented by Sima Qian out of nowhere. Their historical traces could be found. In "The Biographies of the Dawan," "The Annals of Yu the Great" is quoted, which demonstrates that there had been such a kind of writing in the past. The "Dieji" and "Chun Qiu Li Pu Die" mentioned in the "Genealogical Table of the Three Ages" and "The Chronological Table of the Feudal Lords" must be chronological tables, or records of major events. In "The House of Wei Kangshu," there are texts such as "I have read the Houses," which also suggests a book such as Feudal Houses. Even though Sima Qian did not invent all these categories, we must still give him credit for what he has created. He was like a great architect, transforming all rudimentary forms of buildings into a grand palace. The "treatise" is a great example of Sima Qian's work. Some researchers believe that this form of writing already existed before. *The Book of History—Tributes of Yu* records information of mountains, rivers and the produce of places. *The Book of Rites* records the rituals of ceremonies and music. These books could be regarded as the origins of Sima Qian's "treatises." However, the eight Treatises written by Sima Qian cover a large scope of things with detailed procedures, which is far beyond *Tributes of Yu's* reach. With the creation of this category, history books in China started to record not only human behaviours, they also provided background information on the economy and people's thought of these times. This is very important for historical research. Without doubt, the *Shiji* gives the best description of the people of those times. "Biography" is another of Sima Qian's great creation. He divided the biographies into four groups, namely, biography (of one person), combined biography (of two or more people), special categories (which record people of

因其是起义的发难者，"其所置遣侯王将相竟亡秦"，所以，司马迁也突破传统观念，将他列为世家。

5. "列传"七十篇。列传基本上是人物传记，从先秦至当时，包含甚广。如贵族、将相、策士、政治家、军事家、文学家、经学家、隐士、刺客、酷吏、游侠、循吏、滑稽、卜者、医生、商人等等社会各阶层人物都包含在内。此外《匈奴列传》、《大宛列传》等篇，或叙我国少数民族历史，或叙邻国历史。列传最后一篇为作者自传——《太史公自序》，并附《史记》各篇提要。《自序》最后统计《史记》五种体例"凡百三十篇，五十二万六千五百字"。

据前人研究，《史记》的五种体例都不是凭空产生，而是有其历史渊源的。比如《大宛列传》后，引述了《禹本纪》的话，可见古时有一部称作本纪的书。又如《三代世表叙》、《十二诸侯年表叙》中提到《谍记》、《春秋历谱谍》等，大概也属年表、大事记之类。又如《卫康叔世家》后提到"余读世家言"，也许指一部称作"世家"的古书。虽然有这样一些来历，可是我们必须承认司马迁的伟大创造。就好像各种建筑形式本来都有雏形，但将其集中到一处，形成结构严谨的宏伟壮丽的建筑群，则不能不承认是一位伟大的建筑师的创造一样。在五种体例中尤其"书"这种体例，更是一种了不起的发明。有的研究者认为"书"之一体古代也有。如《尚书·禹贡》专记山川、物产，《礼经》载礼乐制度等。这些固然可说是"书"之起源，但"八书"涉及面那么广，叙述发展过程那么详细，则远非《禹贡》等所可比拟。有了"书"这一体，我国史书就不仅记载历史人物的活动，而且为他们的活动多少提供了经济、文化思想的背景，这对于历史研究，无疑是十分重要的。《史记》中最精彩的当然是人物传记，所以"列传"实在是司马迁的又一项伟大

the same category) and appendixes (which include people who were connected with a main figure). This creation makes the *Shiji* stand out among other historical books in that it helps people to "understand history through men," because researchers can compare different kinds of people from all walks of life, vividly described by Sima Qian, and find out the specific social phenomena of a certain period of time. What is more valuable is that the *Shiji* was written in a time when the Han Dynasty had far-reaching power and influence, and this enabled Sima Qian to preserve the history of the leaders of the ethnic minorities and foreign heads of state, and also to record the history of these ethnic groups and of central Asian countries.

The format of the *Shiji*, that is, the biographical style of history keeping, has a great influence on future historical records. History books using this format have been highly regarded and the consecutive records of each dynasty are put together and named "the formal history."

The *Shiji*, a well-structured history book which covers 3,000 years of history, was not the name given at the beginning. When being referred to, it was often called "the Book of the Grand Scribe" or "the Record of the Grand Scribe." *Shiji*, literally means historical records, is a term for ancient history recorded by scribes and one which Sima Qian mentioned in his book. Later on, due to the fact that Sima Qian's book was well-known, the term *Shiji* became more commonly used to describe this historical record. From the late Eastern Han Dynasty, the term *Shiji* referred only to Sima Qian's work.

The passing down of the *Shiji* has seen many turbulences. According to Ban Gu, the author of *The Chronicles of the Han Dynasty — The Biography of Sima Qian*, when the *Shiji* was completed, ten chapters were missing. But Ban Gu did not mention the titles of the ten chapters. Yan Shigu of the Tang Dynasty wrote a commentary on *The Chronicles of the Han Dynasty*, and he quoted Zhang Yan, a scholar from the Three Kingdoms' Period and said, "After Qian's death, many chapters were lost. They included 'The Annals of Emperor Jing,' 'The Annals of Emperor Wu,' 'The Treatise on Rites,' 'The Treatise on Music,' 'The Treatise on Military Practice,' 'The Chronological Table of Generals of the Han Clan,' 'The Biography of Ri Zhe,' 'The Houses of Three Kings,' 'On Divination' and 'The Biography of Fu Jin.' During the reign of Emperor Cheng and Emperor Yuan, the scholar Chu Shaosun added the chapters on 'The Annals of Emperor Wu,' 'The Houses of Three Kings,' 'On Divination,' and 'The Biography of Ri Zhe.' However the versification of these additions was poor in quality and was not the work of Sima Qian." In the *Shiji*, chapters beginning with "Mr. Chu says" were written by Chu Shaosun, a great scholar in the times of

创造。他根据实际需要，将列传类分为专传（一个人物的传）、合传（两个人物传记合在一起叙述）、类传（分类传记）、附传（以一个人物为主，有关的人附在后面）几种。《史记》的"列传"与后来史书不同的是"藉人以明史"，所以涉及社会各方面、各阶层的代表人物，通过各色人物的生动传记，人们可以比较具体、比较全面地了解那一时代的面貌。尤其可贵的是在盛极一时的汉武帝时代，影响达于远方，使《史记》有可能为当时的少数民族及外国君长写了列传，为我国民族史和古代亚洲史保存了珍贵的史料。

《史记》这种体例即所谓纪传体对后世有深远的影响。因此，后来凡采用这种纪、传体裁的史书，都特别受到尊重。其中将各个朝代连续起来的代表作，被称为"正史"。

《史记》这一部结构谨严的三千年通史，最初并没有定名为"史记"，汉代书籍称引到它，往往称作"太史公书"或"太史公记"。"史记"这一名称原来是泛称古史的，意思是史官所记，司马迁书中也曾用到过。后来因为司马迁的书为大家所熟悉，便将《太史公记》简称为"史记"，于是"史记"就成了专名，专指这一部著作了，这已经是东汉末年的事。

《史记》在流传过程中，经过许多的波折，据《汉书·司马迁传》说：《史记》成书之后，很快便缺失了十篇，"有录无书"。班固并未指明缺少哪十篇，而在唐颜师古为《汉书》所作的注中，却引述三国时人张晏的话说："迁殁之后，亡《景纪》、《武纪》、《礼书》、《乐书》、《兵书》、《汉兴以来将相年表》、《日者列传》、《三王世家》、《龟策列传》、《傅靳列传》。元成之间，褚先生补缺，作《武帝纪》、《三王世家》、《龟策》、《日者传》，言辞鄙陋，非迁之意也。"指出了十篇篇名以及褚先生补作情况。这位褚先生，名少孙，是西汉元帝、成帝时的博士。在

Emperor Cheng and Emperor Yuan. Some researchers have different opinions regarding Chu's additions. Wang Mingsheng, a scholar in the Qing Dynasty, who wrote the book *Issues in the Seventeen History Books*, argued that it was "The Annals of Emperor Wu" that was lost and the remaining chapters were copied by Chu from "The Treatise on the Fengshan Ceremony." "The Houses of Three Kings," "The Biography of Ri Zhe" and "On Divination" were not completed by Sima Qian. And there are no traces of other chapters being lost. It is certain that changes have been made to the *Shiji*. Some texts even show events that occurred after Sima Qian's death. How much has been changed, or added, is another topic for research.

Even though there are changes, and sections lost, a relatively complete *Shiji* has been passed down and preserved. Two thousand years have gone by and it still keeps its glory. Nothing can destroy it. This is how the *Shiji* has been accepted by the people.

II The Spirit of "Writing Down Exactly What Happened"

Sima Qian thought that when compiling the *Shiji*, he was continuing the great work of *The Spring and Autumn Annals*, by Confucius. In the "Postface," Sima Qian said, his father had said, "Confucius appeared five hundred years after the death of King Wen of Zhou. It has been five hundred years now since the death of Confucius. Who can carry on the great works of Confucius, and carry on the spirit of *The Book of Odes*, *The Book of History*, *The Book of Rites* and *The Book of Music*? Be alert!" "How could I decline such a great responsibility?" Sima Qian was ready to take on this task. He went on and recorded a dialogue between himself and senior minister Hu Sui. Hu Sui asked, why did Confucius write *The Spring and Autumn Annals*? Sima Qian responded that Confucius' intention was to praise the good and denounce the evil, and also to rescue the chaotic society. Hu Sui pressed on and asked Sima Qian that, Confucius compiled *The Spring and Autumn Annals* because he was then in a chaotic society. Why then are you, in this prosperous time of a sage emperor, writing and following his book? Sima Qian answered, *The Spring and Autumn Annals* is not only criticism. It does contain praise. Being an historian in this prosperous time of a sage emperor, I must praise the merits of the emperor. Besides, all I am doing is editing and compiling, not creating. You are completely wrong in comparing me to Confucius. It seemed Sima Qian's words were self-contradicting, yet he still kept them in the "Postface." Why? He purposefully kept this conversation in it and exposed his determination to

《史记》中有"褚先生曰"开头的，便是他的手笔。关于褚少孙补作的情况，后来也有不同的意见。清代王鸣盛在其《十七史商榷》中便认为，只有《武帝本纪》全亡，是褚少孙抄录《封禅书》来补充的，《三王世家》和《日者》、《龟策》两篇列传，都是没写完，只能说有缺，不能说全篇亡佚，其他各篇则更看不出亡佚的痕迹。《史记》经过后人的补充、改动是可以肯定的。其中有时还提到司马迁死后的事情。至于补充、改动了哪些地方，则是须要进一步研究的课题。

《史记》虽在流传过程中有所散佚，有所改动，但其基本面貌是相当完整地保存了下来。二千年的岁月没有磨去它的光焰，各种灾祸也未能将它销毁，可见这是一部怎样地深入人心的著作了。

（二）"实录"精神

司马迁认为他写作《史记》，是继承孔子修《春秋》的事业。在《太史公自序》中，他说：先父（指司马谈）曾说：周公死后，五百年而有孔子，孔子死后，到现在又有五百年了。谁能继承孔子的事业，保持《诗》、《书》、《礼》、《乐》的精神，千万要在意啊！我怎么敢推辞这样的重任呢？他大有当仁不让的气概。然而在这段话之后，司马迁又记叙了上大夫壶遂与他的一段对话。壶遂问他，孔子何为而作《春秋》？他答以褒善贬恶，拨乱世反之正等等意思。于是壶遂进一步问道，孔子处于乱世故而作《春秋》，你今天处于圣明之世，模仿《春秋》的目的何在呢？他回答说："唯唯，否否。不然！"接着申述《春秋》也有赞美，并非一味刺讥。现在生当圣明之世，我执掌史官，理应歌颂圣德。再说，我所做的不过是编辑、整理，并非创作，你比之作《春秋》，完全错了。看起来司马迁的话

follow the example of the writing of *The Spring and Autumn Annals*, that under an authoritarian dictatorship, it would be difficult to write a history book which both praised and criticised the emperors, yet he would not give up.

Since the *Shiji* praises and criticises the emperors, does this mean it distorts the real events in history? Scholars of the Han Dynasty had already answered this question. Ban Gu said in *The Chronicles of the Han Dynasty— The Biography of Sima Qian*, that, great scholars Liu Xiang and Yang Xiong, both knowledgeable and well-read, praised Sima Qian as a great historian. They admired Sima Qian's excellent descriptions of issues, thorough yet not flowery, down to earth yet not vulgar. They said Sima Qian's articles were straightforward and truthful. He would not praise nor hide erroneous acts. He wrote down exactly what happened. According to the above records, we know that Han scholars regarded the *Shiji* to be solid and well-founded. Its descriptions are truthful, and are called *Shilu*, the record of the truth. Ban Gu further pointed out that Sima Qian relied on books such as *The Annals compiled by Zuo*, *The History of Different States*, *The Book of Lineages*, *The Records of the Warring States*, and *The Annals of Chu and Han*. With great collections of books in the imperial library, Sima Qian would have had access to historical materials beyond those described above. And this is why he could have compiled the *Shiji* which embraces all information and was able to make it a work of great influence.

Faced with so much information, Sima Qian would have had to make decisions as to what to use and what not to use. He was very cautious on this. In the Foreword to "The Biography of Bo Yi," Sima Qian said, "A scholar who possesses a good collection of material still needs to seek confirmation from the six classics." The six classics, namely *The Book of Odes*, *The Book of History*, *The Book of Rites*, *The Book of Changes*, *The Spring and Autumn Annals* and *The Book of Music*, are Confucian books which were highly regarded in the Han Dynasty and regarded as classics. Many ancient historical information was recorded in these six classics. Even though the information may not be fully reliable, it would contain a degree of accuracy, as the Confucian scholars had the characteristic of attaching a greater importance to deeds than to thoughts. Actually, Sima Qian never relied purely on records in books. He relied more on site investigation. For example, according to Zhang Qian, who explored the origin of the Yellow River, there were no Spring Li and Pond Yao in Mount Kunlun as were described in *The Annals of Yu the Great*.

有点前言不搭后语，却又偏偏记在《自序》里，这是什么缘故呢？他实在是欲盖而弥彰，有意透露出在专制的重压下，想要效法《春秋》，写出一部真实的而又含有刺讥褒贬的历史著作真是太难了，但他决不会放弃。

《史记》既然意含刺讥褒贬，那么会不会有损其历史的真实性呢？关于这个问题，汉代的学者早作了回答。班固在《汉书·司马迁传》赞中说：刘向、扬雄学问很大，博览群书，他们都称赞司马迁具备优秀史官的素质。佩服他善于叙述事理，透彻而不求华丽，质朴而不低俗。他的文章率直，记事真实，不妄加好评，也不隐瞒过恶，所以称之为实录。可见汉代的学者都承认《史记》的材料是有根据的，叙述是实事求是的，故而称之为"实录"。班固还指出，汉代以前的历史书，司马迁所依据的便有《左传》、《国语》、《世本》、《战国策》、《楚汉春秋》等书。当然，司马迁所掌握的史料，决不止这几种。"百年之间，天下遗文古事，没有不集中到太史公那里的"，朝廷的藏书以及实际调查之所得——他掌握的史料是相当丰富的。所以《史记》也可说是集大成的著作。

司马迁掌握了相当丰富的史料，便有个辨别取舍的问题，对此，他是很慎重的。在《伯夷列传》序论中，他提到"学者虽然掌握了很多的书籍资料，但还要从六经中求得证明。"六经即经儒家传授，在汉代被抬高到了经典地位的《诗》、《书》、《礼》、《易》、《春秋》、《乐》等六种古代典籍。这些古籍的真正价值在于保存了许多古代的史料，这些史料虽未必完全可靠，但由于儒家重人事轻玄想的特点，总还是比较实在的。其实，司马迁并不仅仅根据书本来考信，可以说他更重视实地调查。比如在《大宛列传》赞中，他便根据张骞探寻河源，并未看到像《禹本纪》上所讲有醴泉瑶池的昆仑山，从而否定了《禹本

Because of this, in "The Biographies of the Dawan," Sima Qian corrected the records in *The Annals of Yu the Great,* and also in *The Classic of Mountains and Rivers (Shanhai Jing).* This is just an example of how Sima Qian tested information recorded in the book with the real facts on site. It was Sima Qian's wish that all things recorded must be truthful. However, because of the times he was in and the fact that he was still subject to some superstition and sometimes even absurd historical thoughts, his book could not be perfect and fully truthful. There are a few places where discrepancies and repetitions appear. Zhang Zhao of the Qing Dynasty explained the reasons in three points. Firstly, Sima Qian's attitude was to keep what he believed and also to keep what he doubted, as ancient history could not be verified or negated. Sima Qian was very cautious on this. Secondly, Sima Qian compiled the history in the *Shiji* up to his times. Later scholars, like Chu Shaosun, added some texts, which made the book look inconsistent. Thirdly, Sima Qian put criticism and praise in his book; the messages are subtle and may not be understood properly by others. Comments by such scholars as those mentioned made it even harder to comprehend the *Shiji.* One could agree with Zhang Zhao's explanations. For a book that covers three thousand years of history, it would be understandable to have some contradictions and inconsistencies. Sima Qian found some complex situations himself. He said in "The Biography of Su Qin" that there were many descriptions of Su Qin, and many incidents which took place at other times, or some similar incidents, were recorded as if they happened to Su Qin. The stories of Su Qin recorded on a piece of silk unearthed in 1973, in number 3 tomb at *Mawangdui,* is quite different from the current existing versions of *The Records of the Warring States* and the *Shiji.*

The original intention of the *Shiji* was to truthfully record historical events. For example, "The House of Chen She" is a record of the rebellion of Chen Sheng and Wu Guang. Chen and Wu wanted to make the soldiers obey their rules. Chen and Wu wrote "Chen Sheng will be the king" in vermilion on silk and hid it in the belly of a fish someone had caught. When a soldier bought the fish and opened it up, he was amazed to find the writing in the fish. Wu Guang then hid in an old temple where the soldiers camped, lit some fires and cried out imitating foxes, saying, "The Great Chu will rise again. Chen Sheng will be the king." The soldiers were all scared. The next day they kept talking about this with many a side-long glance at Chen Sheng. Wu Guang also made some arrangements and caused some public outrage, and he killed an officer. He then called on the rest to rise up in arms. The Qin's rule was very severe. The soldiers, with the task of transferring prisoners, could not make it in time

纪》、《山海经》的记载，这是利用最新实地调查来验证古书的实例。从司马迁的愿望来说，他是力求真实的，但由于时代的局限，他不可能摆脱某些迷信，甚至某些荒谬的历史观念，因此他的书不可能尽善尽美，也不可能完全真实。就书中记事来看也还有不少前后矛盾互相重复的地方，关于这一点，清代的张照分析其原因，举出三点：一是司马迁采取"信以传信，疑以传疑"的态度，古史渺茫，不敢武断，两存其说，以供参考，这正是司马迁的慎重。二是《史记》写到司马迁当时为止，有缺有不足，褚少孙以下为之补作，徒增杂乱。三是司马迁作史记含有褒贬的意思，其中述古讽今，微言大义，或为后人所不知，因而妄为增益或妄加批评，使得《史记》的本意更加难解了。张照分析的这三点，有一定的道理。总之限于当时的条件，一部上下三千年的通史，出现一些前后矛盾，各篇叙述不完全一致的地方，是可以理解的。司马迁自己也曾发现史料错杂的情形，他在《苏秦列传》赞中说：世人讲苏秦多有不同，不是当时的事情有与之相类似的，都归到了苏秦的名下。1973年长沙马王堆三号汉墓中，发现的帛书，所载苏秦事迹与今本《战国策》及《史记》所载很不相同，正足以说明"多异"的实际情况。

《史记》的本意是力求如实地记载历史事件。比如《陈涉世家》记陈胜、吴广起义的过程。他们商议要在士卒中树立威信，于是用丹砂在帛上写"陈胜王"三个字，放进别人打到的鲜鱼肚子里。士卒买鱼剖开一看，竟有这样的帛书，大为怪异。吴广又藏到暂住地旁的古庙中，烧起几堆野火，装着狐狸叫，像是说"大楚兴，陈胜王"，搞得士卒整夜惊怕。白天，议论纷纷都指指点点看着陈胜。吴广又作了一些布置，激起众怒，当场将押解戍卒的尉官杀死，随即就号召大家起义。秦朝

due to heavy rain, and they would be executed. Even if they could make it in time, 60% to 70% of them would die on the frontier, too. So many of the soldiers wanted to take the chance and support a great cause. Chen Sheng and Wu Guang were only two low-ranking officers and they needed to win trust and support on such supernatural arrangements. When Liu Bang became the Emperor later, he also did similar things. The legend had it that he was a descendant of a dragon and was born after a dragon had intercourse with his mother. There was another legend which said that he once killed a white snake on Mount Mangdang where later people saw an old lady crying, who said that the son of the Red Emperor had killed her son, the son of the White Emperor, and then the old lady disappeared. While Sima Qian did not dispute these legends, his doubt could be read between the lines. Peasant rebellions that took place later also employed similar mystical events to gain popularity. However, Sima Qian was writing about what Chen Sheng did, which certainly exposed the nature of such events.

The *Shiji* truthfully recorded what happened. It "did not give unjustifiable praise, nor did it hide any evil." Sima Qian had his own likes and dislikes amongst the historical figures, but, being an historian, he had to be objective. He would not beautify anyone and wouldn't deliberately hide anything. Xiang Yu and Li Guang were both famous heroes with tremendous military contributions; Sima Qian praised them highly and showed his compassion towards them. At the same time, Sima Qian pointed out their mistakes without mercy. The inhumane behaviour of Empress Lü, an insidious woman, disgusted Sima Qian and he recorded her behaviour in his book. At the same time, Empress Lü had contributed to society, because of her policies to encourage production which led to social stability during the 15 years of her times. Her contributions were also recorded in the *Shiji*. Sima Qian also detested harsh officials of the time and he exposed them all in "The Biographies of Cruel Officials." However, he did not disagree with some of them totally. He wrote about Zhi Du's righteousness, Zhao Yu's upholding of the law, and Zhang Tang's debates on issues that were helpful to the country. These three officials were uncorrupted and that's why they did not have any wealth. Whether the term "cruel officials" should be used for all of them is questionable, as they have their own incentive, and the results of their actions were different.

的严刑竣法逼得人们没有活路，戍卒遇雨误期得死，即使到了戍所，也会死掉十之六七，左右是个死，还不如干它一番大事业。陈胜、吴广，不过是戍卒中的小头目，必须装神弄鬼才能得到九百名戍卒的信任与拥护。汉高祖刘邦起义时，也弄过这些玄虚，传说他是龙种，是他母亲和天龙交合才生的。又说他曾在芒砀山杀死一条白蛇，人们便看到一个老妇人在那里啼哭，说是赤帝子杀了我的儿子白帝子，说完就忽然不见了。对这种传说，司马迁未敢直接说出真相，但字里行间也露出了怀疑。后世农民起义也常伴随着此类神话。既有《陈涉世家》的客观描写，这类故事的底蕴就彻底暴露了，让人们可以有一个清醒的认识。

具有实录精神的《史记》，确也做到了"不虚美，不隐恶"。司马迁对于历史人物有自己的爱憎，笔锋也常带感情。但历史记录需要客观公正，所以在《史记》中，既不会刻意美化，也不会故意隐瞒。项羽、李广都是有很大功劳的英雄人物，司马迁对他们有赞扬，有同情，但对他们的缺点、过错，也毫不留情地予以记载批评。对于阴险狠毒的吕后，司马迁极为反感，对于她种种丧失人性的行为，都一一予以披露。但是在她当政的十五年间，采取了恢复生产，稳定社会秩序的政策，取得了较好的效果，对此，《史记》也并未予以抹煞。酷吏是司马迁深恶痛绝的，但在《酷吏列传》中，除了记述酷吏的惨酷暴虐，对其中的某些人并没有完全否定。如写郅都的刚直，赵禹的据法守正，张汤辩论事情当行不当行，对国家也是有利的。这三人也都能廉洁自守，家无余财。酷吏，从其动机与效果看，也是有所区别的，不能一概而论。

Ⅲ Brilliant Knowledge of History

Knowledge on historical events is very important for an historian. Liu Zhiji, the author of *Shitong*, a historian of the Tang Dynasty said that, to be able to write history, one should have three qualities: talent, learning and knowledge. Not many people can have all three qualities and that is why not many people can write history. The *Shiji* is a book with strong view points and good debates. The profound knowledge illustrated in the *Shiji* raises it beyond any "formal history" written by the historians after Sima Qian's time.

What historical knowledge did Sima Qian have?

Firstly, Sima Qian wrote about men and their activities in history. He said that out of 52 Marquis Kings in the Spring and Autumn Period, 36 were murdered. Countless small states were conquered. What was the reason? The reason was that there was a lack of benevolence in the rulers. The leaders of the states did not win the hearts of their people. Sima Qian did not lay blames for the collapse of a dynasty on heavenly will.

Even since the pre-Qin Period, there had been a theory of divine will, a theory later expanded by Dong Zhongshu and which became mainstream thought in the Han Dynasty. Dong said Heaven had its will and claimed that the power of emperors was bestowed by Heaven. He explained that all natural phenomena such as earthquakes, eclipses of the sun and moon were divine warnings. This theory, on the one hand, deceived people, and on the other hand, helped control the rulers. Mr. Lu Xun said, the emperor, son of heaven, should do things that satisfied Heaven, and should not muck around. If the emperor did outrageous things, Heaven would retaliate with a warning.

Dong's theory became very popular and Sima Qian went to seek advice from him, and it should not seem strange that Sima Qian accepted this theory. In some chapters of the *Shiji*, Sima Qian mentioned the divine theory, especially when talking about astrology. The development of science was not so advanced that it could not get rid of the bondage created by superstition, and sometimes science needed superstition to provide protection. As a humanistic historian, Sima Qian had a goal to "find out the truth of Heaven and men," which led him to have doubts about the relationship between Heaven and men. Sima Qian reserved his attitude towards some superstitious theories. For

（三） 卓越的史识

对于一个历史学家来说，"史识"是非常重要的。唐代著名的史学理论家，《史通》的作者刘知几说：作史应有三种重要的特长，那就是才、学、识。世上的人很少能够兼有，所以作史的人才是很少的。可见史识非常重要。《史记》是一部观点鲜明，议论深刻的书，卓越的史识，使它远远超过后世官修的"正史"。

司马迁有哪些卓越的史识呢？

第一，他写史，是以人为本，主要记载人们的实践活动。他认为春秋时期有五十二个诸侯国灭亡，三十六个国君被杀，被吞并的小国更是数都数不过来，什么原因呢？都是因为失去了根本。这根本就是仁义，就是民心。他没有将历史上的盛衰兴亡归之于天意、天道。

从先秦以来，就流行着天人感应学说，这种学说经过汉武帝时大儒董仲舒的阐扬、改造，成了汉代的主流思想。董仲舒将天说成是有意志的，鼓吹帝王的权力是天帝给与的。并大力宣传有所谓"灾异谴告"，他将山崩地震、日蚀、月蚀等异常的自然现象，都解释成上天发出的谴责、警告。这种天人感应说，一方面是对人民的欺骗，另一方面也多少起了约束统治者的作用。鲁迅就说过儒士讲天，是因为"据说天子的行事，是都应该体贴天意，不能胡闹的"。皇帝闹得太过分了，便抬出天来吓唬吓唬他，请他收敛一点。

董仲舒的学说风靡一时，司马迁曾向董仲舒求教过，所以他接受天人感应的学说是不奇怪的。在《史记》的一些篇章中，尤其是讲到天象历法时，都讲到了天人相应。当时的科学发展还不可能摆脱迷信的束缚，同时也还要靠迷信来保驾护航。但是作为一个以人为本的史学家，司马迁提出了"究天人之际"

example, in "The Biography of Assassins," it was recorded that when Dan, the crown prince of the State of Yan, was a hostage in Qin, and requested to return to his own country, the King of Qin said, "I would let you return when the heavens rain grain and horns grow on horses." Crown prince Dan looked up to the heavens and prayed sincerely, and it rained grain and horns grew on horses. Thus he was returned to his home country. Later on, a book titled "Dan, the Crown Prince of the State of Yan" was circulated and made the event more colourful. Sima Qian did not believe this ridiculous story and criticised its "exaggeration." Zhang Qian, who went to the great west of the country, explored the origin of the Yellow River. According to Zhang Qian's findings, Sima Qian concluded that the Spring Li and Pond Yao or any fairies described in *The Annals of Yu the Great* and *The Classic of Mountains and Rivers* did not exist. Sima Qian claimed that he did not want to follow wrong records. It was Sima Qian's opinion that the fate of one person was determined by the environment he lived in. In "The Biographies of Bian Que and Chunyu Yi," Sima Qian commented that the imperial court was a place full of jealousy. Bian Que, a famous physician, was killed by the imperial physician of the Qin. Chunyu Yi, also a famous physician, was wrongfully charged and was even at the point of execution. His daughter wanted to sell herself in order to buy back her father. When Emperor Wen of the Han heard about the story, he abolished the corporal punishment. Both Bian Que and Chunyu Yi were set up and persecuted because of their fame as excellent physicians. Laozi said, "Beautiful objects are the cause of misfortune." Misfortune was inflicted by the environment, and had nothing to do with fate or heavenly connections. The First Emperor of the Qin conquered the six states and built a powerful Qin Dynasty. His empire was overthrown over ten years later by peasant rebels. Later on, Xiang Yu, who became an overlord who ruled a vast area with strong armies, was defeated less than three years later by Liu Bang whose forces were much weaker than Xiang's. Why? Jia Yi of the Han Dynasty wrote an article "on the Errors Committed in the Qin Dynasty" (Guoqinlun) and he pointed out that "Qin did not have benevolent rule and there was a change in the methods of attack and defense." Sima Qian agreed with Jia Yi's comments and cited the whole article in "The Annals of the First Emperor of the Qin." In Sima Qian's opinion, the First Emperor of the Qin and Xiang Yu were powerful persons who relied on force under their rule. They lacked the support of the people, and

的目标。他要探究天人之间的实际情形，结果是对天人关系表示了很大的怀疑。他对一些迷信、怪异的说法，都持批评怀疑的态度。比如《刺客列传》中，说到世人传说燕国的太子丹，在秦国做人质时，曾要求回国，秦王说：你要能让天上落下粮食，马头上长出角来，就放你回国。太子丹仰天而叹，感动了上天，竟然"天雨粟，马生角"，因而被放归。后来有一本叫《燕丹子》的书，更将这事说得活灵活现。司马迁不取这一荒诞传说，并批评说"太过"。当时，通西域的张骞曾经实际考察了黄河的源头。司马迁根据他考察的结果，指出《禹本纪》《山海经》记载的昆仑山上有醴泉、瑶池和种种神怪都是没有的，说，我可不敢跟着乱说。司马迁认为人生的命运，往往是环境造成的。在《扁鹊仓公列传》的"太史公曰"中，司马迁写道："女无美恶，居宫见妒，士无贤不肖，入朝见疑"，宫内、朝廷就是你争我夺的妒忌场。扁鹊因为医术高明，被秦朝的太医令派人刺杀了。仓公就是太仓令淳于意，也因医术高明，被人诬告，将要受刑，多亏他的小女儿缇萦上书，要以身为奴婢救赎父亲，这件事感动了汉文帝，宣布要废止肉刑。扁鹊、仓公都因医术高妙而受到迫害，真如老子所说："美好者，不祥之器"，美好的事物会招来妒忌，引起争端，所以是不吉利的。祸患来自人世，是现实环境造成的，和天命、天道全无关系。秦始皇吞并六国，建立了统一强大的秦王朝，但不过十几年，就被揭竿而起的平民推翻。楚汉之际，项羽兵强地广，成为发号施令的霸主，但不到三年，即被远为弱小的刘邦消灭。什么原因呢？关于秦亡，汉初的贾谊写了一篇《过秦论》，提出是因为"仁义不施而攻守之势异也"。司马迁同意他的观点，在《秦始皇本纪》后面，全引了这篇文章。司马迁认为秦始皇和项羽，都自恃武力，施暴政而不行仁义，失去民心，所以失败，

that was the reason for their defeat. Sima Qian's doubt about the divine theory was clearly manifested in "The Biography of Bo Yi," where good people suffered short lives or even starved to death, and evil people enjoyed luxury and wealth. Sima Qian asked, "Is this divine intention or is it not?"

In Sima Qian's time, due to the limitation of science, and even more to the propaganda of the rulers, the public succumbed to superstition. However, practice teaches. By observation and the study of historical events, Sima Qian concluded that the divine theory could not be relied on, and this was the reason that he was able to write such a great book on humanity.

Secondly, Sima Qian studied history from a unique angle. He suggested that he should follow the link of changes throughout history. *The Book of Changes* had a great effect on him and he recognised the constant change in everything. The change of dynasty was also a natural occurrence. He wanted to "observe the history of each dynasty at its beginning and tell the end," he also wanted to "see the peak of a dynasty and know the fall." He had found some of the clues to the trends of dynasties. He realized that when society became poor, and the lives of the people worsened, there would be a need for change. Also, he realized that when a dynasty reached its peak, it would also be the time of going down. He found the changes took place gradually. For example, the unification that Xia, Shang and Zhou achieved in their respective history was the effort of many generations. At the same time, the fall of a dynasty was not because of one day's error. A further example is the Qin Dynasty which conquered all six other big states and united the whole country. It all started with Duke Xiang of Qin and it took many generations to achieve unification. Sima Qian, basing his claims on the ideas of change, suggested that when time changed, a lot of measures should be changed, too.

Sima Qian's emphasis on "seeing the peak of a dynasty and knowing the fall" was based on the real situation of the time. During Emperor Wu's reign, the Han Dynasty was at its peak. There were some signs of decline. Sima Qian saw all of these. In "The Treatise on Equalization" he described that when a dynasty underwent change, a historical figure would also be changed subsequently. For example, when Liu Bang, the Emperor Gaozu of the Han, who had been a hooligan-like local chief in Si River, became a poetic emperor who sang the "Song of Great Wind," and created a new dynasty, there had been

天命起不了任何作用。司马迁对于"天道"的怀疑，突出地表现在《伯夷列传》中，他根据现实生活中，好人或者短命或者穷饿而死，而恶人却得享荣华富贵的事实，提出"倘所谓天道，是邪，非邪？"公正的赏善罚恶的天道在哪里？

司马迁生活的时代，由于科学发展水平的限制，更由于统治者的大力宣扬，人们被包围在封建迷信的浓雾之中。但实践会使人变得聪明起来，司马迁通过对历史和现实的考察，得出了天道不足信的结论，这样才完成了一部以人为本的历史。

第二，司马迁是用变化的观点来考察历史的。他提出要"通古今之变"，就是说要贯通从古到今的变化发展。他受《易经》的影响，认为事物都是不断变化的，因此，历史上的朝代也不断地更替着。他著《史记》就是要"原始察终，见盛观衰"，就是说要考察一个王朝是怎样兴起又怎样灭亡的。他从历史发展中发现了一些规律。他认识到，世道穷困，民生凋敝，就会要求改变。而当一个王朝发展到极盛时，往往也就是衰败的开始，事物总是到了极点也就开始了新的转化。他还认识到盛衰的演变是由"渐"而成的。比如夏、商、周能够实现天下一统，都是经过了许多代的努力。后来演变成乱世，也不是一朝一夕造成的。再如秦王朝，最终由秦始皇灭掉六国实现统一，也是从秦襄公开始，多少代努力的结果。从"变"的观点出发，司马迁认为时代变化了，许多措施也都应该与旧时不同。

司马迁强调"见盛观衰"，也是针对当时的。汉武帝时代，曾达到极盛的地步，但也出现了衰败的契机。这是司马迁所亲见的。在《平准书》中，他颇有预见性的详细地予以记述。一个王朝一个时代在变，一个历史人物在其一生中也会有很多的变化。比如汉高祖刘邦。从一个颇有一些无赖习气的泗上亭长到高唱《大风歌》的开国君王，其性格、行为无疑都有一个质

many changes. Many detailed descriptions can be found in the *Shiji*.

Thirdly, Sima Qian believed that "heroes were made in the right times," and not that "heroes made the times." During the Warring States Period, many people of low social status were able to rise to become prime ministers; in the rebellious times at the end of the Qin's rule, many heroes emerged. Liu Bang, the Emperor Gaozu of the Han, was only a local chief when he took up arms. Those who followed him were merely civilians in humble jobs. They took the opportunity and rose with Liu Bang, and in the end they helped bring about a great unification. The first to take up arms was Chen Sheng. He said even before that "There are no born princes, barons, generals and ministers." He, like many, did not believe in the divine theory and he rose up and changed his own fate, and even changed the fate of the country.

Fourthly, Sima Qian had pity on the loser and the hero that failed. A fair historian would not judge a person by whether he succeeded or not. For Sima Qian, the most important thing was to find out the reason for the failure. In the *Shiji*, Sima Qian showed sympathy for the tragic endings of Xiang Yu, Han Xin and Li Guang. A hero, according to Sima Qian, did not have to be a person of great influence. In "The Biographies of the Wandering Knights," Sima Qian sang highly of those figures in daily life who honoured their words and would even sacrifice their lives to help others who were in danger. These people were people of low social status and could rely on no political or economical influence. They relied on their own capability to have their names known. They, echoed by those figures shown in *Outlaws of the Marsh*, were righteous people and would help others in danger, and they would not receive money in gratitude. According to Sima Qian, these gallant citizens were different from those hooligans in society who had some power and bullied others. Sima Qian wrote about some wandering knights in "The Biographies of the Assassins" like Cao Mo, Nie Zheng and Jing Ke, and praised them for their trustworthiness. They made vows and they honoured them with their actions. They helped the weak and went against the strong, which was also admirable.

Finally, Sima Qian paid attention to the development of the economy and

的飞跃。这种种变化，在《史记》中都有准确、生动的反映。

第三，司马迁确认是"时势造英雄"，而不是英雄决定一切。历史事实是，战国时代许多处于下层的士人，凭三寸不烂之舌便可以立致卿相。到了秦汉之际，在起义的大浪潮中，涌现了许多英雄人物，汉高祖本人不过是个亭长，跟随他起义，后来成为著名的文臣武将的，有许多都曾从事低贱的行业，他们乘势而起，最后竟完成了开创一代兴盛王朝的大业。第一个举起义旗的陈胜，在起义前夕就曾说过"王侯将相宁有种乎？"谁说大人物都应该是世袭的？什么天命说、血统说全是骗人的鬼话！乘势而起，就能改变自己的命运，甚至改变国家的命运。

第四，同情弱者，同情失败的英雄。公正的史家是不以成败论英雄的。在司马迁看来，重要的是找出所以失败的原因。《史记》中，对于项羽、韩信、李广这些结局悲惨的人物，都寄予了较多的同情。在司马迁看来，英雄的标准，倒不必是叱咤风云的人物。他写作《游侠列传》，赞扬的便是一些生活在闾巷中的人物。这些人言必信，行必果，应允的事情一定要做到。他们不顾自己的身家性命，去救助处于危难的人。这些闾巷、乡曲之侠，都是出身于下层的人物，没有现成的政治、经济地位可以凭借。全是靠自己卓越的行为来树立声名。他们就像《水浒传》所写"担着血海也似干系"，见义勇为，救人危难而又不肯受报的慷慨之士。在司马迁的笔下，"乡曲之侠"与那些侵凌孤弱，恣欲自快的豪暴之徒是完全不同的，那些人只是一些恶霸流氓，不配算作游侠。司马迁还写了《刺客列传》，表扬了曹沫、聂政、荆轲等人，说他们立下的志愿光明磊落，并且始终都没有辱没所立的志愿。他们不顾生命助弱抗强，也值得人们敬佩。

第五，重视经济的发展和生产活动。《史记》中《平准书》

production. "The Treatise on Equalization" and "The Biographies of Usurers" in the *Shiji* are Sima Qian's articles on economy. In the latter, Sima Qian attached great importance to the economy. He quoted Guanzi, who said, "When the barn is full, people start to know rituals; When the dress and food are sufficient, people start to understand honour and disgrace." The rituals could only be practised when the people have some economic security. Sima Qian used the example of the State of Qi. When Jiang Ziya was once conferred in Yingqiu where the land was barren and the population was sparse, Jiang encouraged his people to take up other productive activities, such as fishing, salt manufacturing, textiles, embroidery, and expanded trades. He made Qi very wealthy and powerful. Later, Qi declined before Duke Huan of Qi came to power. Duke Huan appointed Guan Zhong as the prime minister and encouraged these activities. He later became one of the Overlords. Sima Qian pointed out that the four major industries, namely agriculture, tradesman-ship, commerce and *Yu* (industries related to wild life products, forests, marshes and waters), were the basis from which the people got their daily necessities, and on which to build a strong country, and that the ideology of "small state with few people" was outdated. Material wealth and power had become the public desire which had been driving productivity. "People come and go all for the sake of benefit and self interest." This is a situation that should not be suppressed, and must not be forbidden. Rulers should only provide guidance, satisfy their needs, and lead the public onto the right track.

Commerce, on the one hand, promoted productivity, and on the other hand, debased social morality. The power of money was everywhere, of which Sima Qian had vivid descriptions. In his time, whoever had money could pay and become government officials. Those who committed crimes could offset their sentences by paying money. Hence there was a saying, "Sons of wealthy people won't have to be executed in the public market." Because of this, more people fanatically pursued the accumulation of money. Sima Qian had his own first hand experience. When he was thrown into prison, he could not get any help because he was poor and without social status. He hated the unjust society in which only money was almighty. He despised those Confucian scholars who showed contempt when talking about money and profit. It was his opinion that those scholars did not have outstanding virtue and capabilities. They lived in society yet they were poor and not able to make ends meet for their families. They were not even able to prepare for the offerings to their ancestors. How ridiculous it would be for these people to talk about benevolence and virtue!

Sima Qian attached great importance to economic development. He

和《货殖列传》都是讲经济问题的。在《货殖列传》中，司马迁强调了经济生活的重要。他引述管子的话说："仓廪实而知礼节，衣食足而知荣辱"，礼仪道德是要有一定的经济基础作为保证的。他还举出历史上的齐国为例，当太公望封于营丘时，那里土地很差，人民也少，就是靠着提倡渔、盐、纺织、刺绣等生产活动，大力发展商业，使得齐国日益富强起来的。后来齐国衰弱，到齐桓公时，管仲为相，鼓励生产，扩大流通，振兴了齐国，使得齐桓公成为号令诸侯的霸主。司马迁指出：农、工、商、虞（山林泽薮）四种生产活动，是老百姓衣食的来源，增加来源才能够国富民强。司马迁清醒地认识到，"小国寡民"的理想已成遥远的过去，人们追求物质财富，追求权势荣耀，已成为普遍的习俗。欲望刺激生产，"天下熙熙，皆为利来；天下攘攘，皆为利往"，人们奔来走去，都是为了追逐利益。对于这种情形，不能压制，更不能禁止，而只能因势利导，予以适当满足，引导到正确的发展方向上来。

商品经济一方面促进了生产的发展，另一方面却也在毒化着社会风气。金钱的魔力几乎无处不在，对此，《史记》有深刻地揭露，当时社会，只要有了钱，就可以买官买爵，犯了法还可以用钱去赎，所以说："千金之子，不死于市"，这就更刺激了人们疯狂地去追求财富。对于这种种腐败现象，司马迁是感受极深的。在他陷于冤狱时，就因为无财无势而不能得到救助。他痛恨不公正的金钱万能的社会，但他对于羞于言利的迂儒也大不以为然，他批评这些人并没有高尚的节操和卓越的才能，生活在俗世之中，却长期贫困，家里老婆孩子都养不活，逢年过节祭祀祖宗的祭品也准备不起来，却在那里大谈仁义道德，岂不可耻，岂不可笑!

司马迁重视经济发展，对当时汉武帝的经济政策，作了认

analysed the economic policies at the time and commented on them. In " The Treatise on Equalization," Sima Qian criticised Emperor Wu's military ambitions and his pursuit of victories, and his luxurious life style which made the country virtually bankrupt. Then the Emperor put a price tag on official titles. He also made regulations that one could offset his crimes by paying money. These kinds of activities corrupted the officials and made society chaotic. The Emperor also gave orders for the control of salt and iron manufacturing and the minting of money. He applied monopoly principles in business, set restrictions on commerce by using methods of equality of commodities and transportation, and encouraged people to secretly inform on others. A lot of middle class families became bankrupt, the whole commercial sector went down, which led to economic recession. The common people were unable to make ends meet. Sima Qian pointed out that a ruler should provide guidance on the needs of the people. Any forced changes of people's will would be wrong. A ruler should not scramble for profit from its people. However, Emperor Wu just took that road which caused serious problems for his country.

Sima Qian set a very high standard for himself when compiling the *Shiji*. He wanted "to examine all that concerns Heaven and man, to penetrate the changes of the past and present, and complete a work of my own." He kept marching towards his goal. However, like many great thinkers and literati, he had contradictory thoughts. The ideas of the controlling party, as well as traditional perceptions, all had limited him, but, reality of life opened his eyes. He was able to break away from his restrictions and "complete a work of his own." His book, to the people of his time, was truly something "of his own" and is a monumental piece.

真的分析、批评。在《平准书》中，他批评汉武帝连年征战，好大喜功，奢侈靡费，弄到国库空虚。于是便采取各种办法搜括钱财，官职爵位都定价出卖，又规定交纳金钱可以赎罪，搞得官场黑暗，社会风气一塌糊涂。同时，又下令将盐、铁、铸钱收归国有，采取垄断经营，又采用平准、均输、告缗等手段，打击工商业。搞得中等之家大批破产，工商业萎缩，经济衰退，到了民穷财尽的地步。司马迁曾提出，对于民众求富的欲望，只能因势利导，勉强纠正都不是办法，而"最下者与之争"，与民争利是最要不得的，而汉武帝恰恰是采用了这样的政策，自然就危机重重了。

司马迁著《史记》，对自己提出了很高的要求，即"究天人之际，通古今之变，成一家之言"。他不断向着这一目标前进。当然，和古代许多伟大的思想家、文学家一样，他的思想也充满了矛盾。占统治地位的思想，传统的观念也对他起着束缚作用。但生活实践促使他睁开眼睛看世界，在许多方面挣脱了这种束缚，提出了一些独具创造性的观点，成就了"一家之言"。从他所处的那个时代来看，他这一家之言，是可以惊天地而泣鬼神的。

陈胜、吴广起义

The Uprising of Chen Sheng and Wu Guang

I **Historiography and Literature**

A great historical book is also an excellent literary work. This is a common case in ancient Chinese literature. *The Annals Compiled by Zuo, The History of Different States* and *The Records of the Warring States*, are all history books, yet who could deny the literary value of them? The objects of history and literature are society and humanity. In theory, the perspectives from which they describe them are different. Greek historian and poet Aristotle said in his book *Art of Poetry* that "The difference between them is that one talks about things of the past; and the other talks about things that are likely to happen. From this perspective, poems have more philosophical meaning and are more beautiful because poems deal with general truth, while history deals with the specific truth." Aristotle thought that history reflected the truth yet it could not record things that were untrue yet had the possibility of being true. This is why history lacks generality and universality. Nikolay Chernyshevsky, the 19th century Russian thinker, wrote in his book *The Aesthetic Relations of Art to Reality* that "The relation of art to life is the same as that of history; the only difference in content is that history, in its account of the life of mankind, is concerned mainly with factual truth, whereas art gives us stories about the lives of men in which the place of factual truth is taken by faithfulness to psychological and moral truth. The first function of history is to reproduce life; the second, which is not performed by all historians, is to explain it." He explained from a different perspective the differences between the two, that history reflects universality and focuses on society while art reflects individualism and focuses on individuals. The quotes from the two giants complement each other and give rise to thoughts on the similarities and differences between art and history. Chernyshevsky's words further remind us there are a lot of similarities between history and art. When a great literary work describes the lives of individuals, the vast social environment in which the individuals live is naturally described. At the same time, a great historical work which gives vivid descriptions presents the history to the readers with a

（一）史学与文学

一部优秀的历史著作，同时又是一部优秀的文学著作，在我国古代是常有的现象。《左传》、《国语》、《战国策》都是记载历史的书，谁又能否定它们的文学价值呢？历史、文学都是以社会和人为表现对象的，从理论上说，二者表现的角度并不相同。古希腊的亚里士多德曾区别历史学家和诗人说："他们的区别在于：一是述说已然的事物，另一是述说可能的事物。在这一点上讲，诗比历史是更有哲学意味以及更为优美的东西：因为诗主要地关切着的是一般的真理，历史则是特殊的真理。"（《诗学》第二篇六）他认为历史反映的是既成事实，不能表现虽非实有却是可能的事物。因此缺少概括性、普遍性。十九世纪俄国民主主义思想家车尔尼雪夫斯基则曾这样来比较艺术与历史："艺术对生活的关系完全像历史对生活的关系一样，内容上唯一的不同是历史叙述人类的生活，艺术则叙述人的生活；历史叙述社会生活，艺术则叙述个人生活。历史的第一个任务是再现生活；第二个任务——那不是所有的历史学家都能做到的——是说明生活。"（《生活与美学》）他从另一个角度说明二者的区别：历史表现的是共性，着重叙述社会；艺术表现的是个性，着重叙述个人。以上所引的两段话互相补充，对于了解文艺与历史的同异很有启发。车尔尼雪夫斯基的话更提醒我们，历史与文艺是有很多共同性的。一部伟大的文学著作在描写个人生活的同时，不是必然要展现出广阔的社会生活背景吗？同样，一部伟大的历史著作，为使所叙史实能给人鲜明的印象，也必然在可以容许的范围内，尽可能将历史人物写得生动、具体。一般的历史著作只求忠实地记录，但是如果这位史学家同时又是一位思想家，同时又是一位感情丰富的诗人，那

vivid picture. Normally, history books record faithfully historical events. If the historian happened to be a thinker and passionate poet, then his historical book would be different. Not only would the historian explain life in reality, he would also need to express his dreams about life. If this were the case, it would be difficult to tell the history and the art apart. However, history is not to be fabricated, while life itself is colourful with many stereotypes which could be highlighted by an author and his writings and then become a moving story. In ancient Chinese history, there is no clear-cut border between literature, history and philosophy. There are certain requirements for each of the three types of essays in terms of form and content. Some fabricated stories were woven into historical books (as there are many fabricated events in *The Annals Compiled by Zuo* and *The Records of the Warring States*). There is not much fabricated content in the *Shiji*, yet some details might have been created by Sima Qian's imaginations. Sima Qian created the biographical style of history keeping, and in each chapter, he depicted influential historical figures. This history book, when reaching the pinnacle of historical glory, also climbed to the top of literary peak. In his descriptions, Sima Qian illustrated his love and hatred, and also showed his longing for justice and enlightenment. Is this a purely historical record? No, this is a poetic and artistic treasure. It is like the great poem "The Lament" but without rhymes.

II The Outcry Against Injustice

Sima Qian did not only faithfully record historical events in the *Shiji*, he expressed his outcry against injustice, which could be read between the lines, and showed his feeling of love and hatred, compassion and anger. "The Biography of Bo Yi," the first chapter of Biographies series, is very simple. However, Sima Qian wanted to use this simple story to express his views, to ask questions, and to question injustice. He asked, the hermits such as Xu You, Bian Sui and Wu Guang were virtuous people, however, their deeds were seldom found in *The Book of Odes* and *The Book of History*. Why? He mentioned that Confucius said Bo Yi and Shu Qi pursued benevolence and they achieved it, so they should have no complaints. However, a sense of complaint could be found in their poems written before their deaths. Did they complain or not? Sima Qian said that normally, Heaven was just and would help only the good man. Bo Yi and Shu Qi were good men by any standard, yet they starved to death in Shouyang Mountain. Among 72 of Confucius' students, Yan Yuan was the most studious. Yet he was the poorest and had to eat rice bran to live, and he died very young. Why did Heaven cast bad luck on

么，情况就完全不同了。他不仅再现而且还要说明生活，而且还要从中表现他生活的理想。这样历史与艺术便很难区别了，唯一的区别便是历史不允许虚构。可是生活本身就是丰富多彩的，就存在着各种各样的典型，经过作者的点睛之笔，摘出其主要特点，便具有动人的艺术魅力。我国古代文、史、哲没有十分明确的界限，对每一种文体都提出过文（形式）、质（内容）适当的要求。所以甚至在史学著作中也多少加入了虚构成份（《左传》、《战国策》便颇多虚构）。《史记》虚构不多，但在细节描写上，也不能说完全没有想象的成份。由于司马迁创造了纪传体，在每一篇传记中，着力刻画了有影响的历史人物，所以在纪传体的史学著作登上史学殿堂的同时，传记文学也第一次登上了文学的宝座。司马迁写这些人物传记时，爱憎分明，笔含褒贬，倾注了他的不平和对于光明的向往。这仅仅是历史的客观记录吗？不！这是诗，是艺术奇珍，是"无韵之《离骚》"。

（二）抒不平之气

司马迁写作《史记》，并不只是客观地记述历史，而是充满着牢骚不平之气的。这种不平之气回荡在许多篇章的字里行间，勃郁于"太史公曰"的评赞之内，表达了作者的爱与憎，同情与愤慨。列传的第一篇《伯夷列传》所记历史事实极简单，主要是一篇借题发挥的文章，通篇都是疑问，通篇都是不平。他问道：传说中许由、卞随、务光这些岩穴之士德义是很高尚的，但《诗》、《书》中却很少有关于他们的记载，这是什么缘故呢？他问道：孔子说伯夷、叔齐，"求仁得仁，又何怨？"然而，看他们饥饿将死时的诗篇还是很有怨气的。他们到底是怨呢，不怨呢？他问道：通常说天是最公正的，只帮助好人。伯夷、叔齐可算好人了，却饿死在首阳山，孔子七十二弟子中，

such good men? It was said that "Dao Zhi" killed innocent people and ate their livers. Yet, he lived to an old age and died peacefully. What kind of logic was this? Sima Qian said, evil people could enjoy luxurious lives and they could pass down their fortunes to their children, while good people suffered a lot. There were too many such things happening. "What is the law of Heaven? Is it true or is it false?" Sima Qian asked a series of questions. He used the same way as Qu Yuan, the great poet, asked questions in his famous poetry *Tian Wen* (Questions to Heaven). Deep in Sima Qian's mind the popular theory of heavenly laws began to collapse. Sima Qian pointed out in the *Shiji* that it was impossible for commoners to build up their fame with virtuous deeds. They could only rely on famous people. In a society where people attached great importance to money and power, humble people would seek fame in vain. Sima Qian's thoughts, together with the "Letter to Ren An," "The Biographies of Usurers" and "The Biographies of the Wandering Knights" demonstrated his hatred and resentment. It was an amazing thing for him to have such thoughts at that time. Sima Qian was fully aware of the injustice of the feudal society. He expressed his thoughts in the "Biography of General Li." General Li Guang was a capable military figure and was excel in shooting. One day he thought he had caught sight of a tiger. He took out his bow and arrow and shot. Later it was found out that the arrow went into the tiger which turned out to be a rock. General Li was loved by his soldiers because he cared for them. When receiving awards, he would share the money with his subordinates; he would also share meals with them. When his army found water in the deserts, he would not drink unless all of his soldiers had drunk, nor would he eat unless all of his soldiers had eaten. General Li became a soldier in his 20s and fought the Xiongnu. He had fought more than 70 battles and he had gained much military glory. So he was given the title "Flying General of the Han." Such a general as Li, was suppressed later and was not given any official titles. He was even sidelined and persecuted by another general by the name of Wei Qing, and later he committed suicide. Sima Qian had a great deal of sympathy for General Li Guang. After Li Guang's death, he wrote "All of Li's army cried. When the commoners heard it, they, whether knowing or unknowing, old or young, all burst into tears." Sima Qian described the commemoration to show his high

颜渊最好学，但却贫困，常以糟糠充饥，且又早死，天所报答于善人的，又怎样呢？传说"盗跖"残杀无罪的人，拿人肝当肉吃，但却活到老年，平安死去，他遵守的又算什么样的德行呢？他又问道：近世以来恶人终身享受而且传之子孙后代，好人却遭灾遇难，备受打击，这种事太多太多了。那么，"倘所谓'天道'，是邪？非邪？"这一连串的问题，很有点像屈原的《天问》，胸中充满怀疑便以文词表现出来，风靡当时的"天道"说，在司马迁的思想深处动摇了，开始崩溃了。在文章中，他还指出：普通老百姓，要想靠行为高尚来建立声名，那是不可能的，不依附地位高名声大的人士，怎能传名于后世呢！在一个金钱与权势统治的社会里，卑贱者无论怎样上进，怎样努力，也是很难有出路的。将司马迁的这些话与《报任安书》、《货殖列传》、《游侠列传》等对照来看，他的怨愤是极深的。当时能有这种思想感情，的确很了不起。司马迁深切地感到封建社会的种种不平，在他所写的《李将军列传》中，以李广个人不幸的遭遇，作出了更形象的说明。李广射艺高强，曾误以石为虎，一箭射去，整个箭头都陷进了石中。作为一个将军，他非常爱护部下：得到赏赐，就分给部下，和士兵同饮共食。他带兵，走到荒漠的地方，发现了水，士卒没有全部喝到水，他就不去水边；士卒没有都吃到饭，他就不去吃饭。李广从二十岁起和匈奴作战，大小七十余战，屡创奇迹，被匈奴誉为"汉之飞将军"。就是这样一位名将，却始终受压抑不得封侯，最后受到大将军卫青种种掣肘、打击，而悲愤自杀。司马迁对李广是极其同情的。他特意写道，李广自杀后，"广军士大夫一军皆哭，百姓闻之，知与不知，无老壮，皆为垂涕"。用百姓的悼念情景，给这位名将以极高的礼赞。如果我们将《李将军列传》与《卫将军骠骑列传》对照来看，作者的不平

regard for this beloved general. If we compare the "Biography of General Li" and "The Biography of Cavalry General Wei," we can see even more clearly Sima Qian's criticisms of the society of the time. General Huo Qubing, the General of Cavalry, contributed greatly in the battles against the Xiongnu. In the "Biography," Sima Qian repeatedly pointed out the fact that his soldiers and chiefs were the chosen strong ones, because Emperor Wu had equipped General Huo with the best soldiers and paved the road for his success. How did this glorious general treat his soldiers then? When he led his army he had a few chariots of imperial chefs with him in procession. On his way back, he threw away a great deal of good food while many of his soldiers were left to starve. When he was at the frontier, some of his soldiers were weak from starvation, yet General Huo would keep on playing his football games. What a contrast this is between him and General Li Guang! General Wei and General Huo were related to Wei Zifu, the Empress (General Wei was the elder brother of the Empress, while General Huo was her nephew). They both received special attention because of that relationship. Besides, these two generals knew how to please the Emperor as they knew how to "read" the emperor's thoughts. Even though their obsequious behaviour was despised by ministers in the court, they were awarded higher and higher official titles. When Sima Qian wrote "The Biography of Cavalry General Wei," he had General Li Guang in mind. His criticism of General Wei and General Huo was not simply to give vent to his anger.

Sima Qian used his pen to criticise, to express his love and hatred, and to cry out against injustice. In the "Biographies of Qu Yuan and of Master Jia Yi" he said, "Heaven is the origin of humans, and parents are of great importance. When a man is in a desperate situation, he tries to search for his origin and roots. Hence, a man cries to Heaven when in extreme distress, and he cries for his parents when in extreme despair. Qu Yuan, an upright person who served the King of Chu whole-heartedly, was alienated from King of Chu and lost his trust. He was in such a desperate situation. How could he, an honest person who was subject to doubts, not be resentful? He wrote the great poem ' The Lament' out of his anger." Not only is this a record of comments, it also expresses Sima Qian's feelings. In the same biography, there is another discourse, which goes, "A head of state, whether wise or stupid, good or bad, would always wish loyal ministers to support him, and would want to select good ministers to assist him. However, for a long period of time, one dynasty after another fell, and there was no evidence of wise Kings and prosperous

以及对当时社会的批评就更为明显了。霍去病为骠骑将军，在与匈奴作战中他是有功劳的。但传中却一再交代"骠骑所将常选"，"而敢力战深入之士，皆属骠骑"。汉武帝为他配备了很强的部属，并在行军路线上为他创造立功条件，使他得以青云直上。这位贵族公子出身的大将，是怎样对待士卒的呢？他出征时，皇帝派了御厨带着几十辆食品车跟从，他回来的时候，车上丢弃了不少很好的食物，而士卒却有忍饥挨饿的人。在塞外，士卒饿得站不起来，他却照样"穿域蹋鞠"（踢球），并且像这一类事在他是习以为常的。这和李广对待士卒是多么鲜明的对照。然而，卫青、霍去病都是武帝皇后卫子夫的亲属（卫青是卫子夫之兄，霍去病是卫子夫姊子），特别受到宠信。不仅如此，这二人还很善于逢迎，颇能体会武帝心意。能够"以和柔自媚于上"，虽然不为贤士大夫所称誉，官却是越做越大。相信司马迁在写《卫将军骠骑列传》时，李广的形象是活跃在他心中的。他对卫、霍的某些批判、揭露，也是为了一吐不平之气。

　　司马迁笔锋常带感情，在列传中有时发而为议论，表现了他强烈的爱憎，抒写了不平之气。像《屈原贾生列传》中这样一段话："说到天，那是人的源头，说到父母，那是人的根本，人在极其困顿的时候，就会追念根本，所以人在劳苦倦极的时候，就要呼唤老天，在伤痛悲愤的时候，就要呼唤父母。屈平（屈原名平，字原）行为正直，为楚王贡献自己的忠心与才智，但却被小人挑拨，失去了楚王的信任，真是处境艰难了！讲诚信反而被怀疑，尽忠心反而被诽谤，他能不怨愤吗？屈平写作《离骚》，就是由于怨愤而产生的啊！"这段话是评论，也是发挥。同一篇中还有这样一段话：一个国君，不管是聪明还是愚笨，是好是坏，总还希望有忠臣支持他，选拔贤臣来辅助他，

countries. The reason for this is that many heads of state believed themselves to be wise leaders but in fact were not. Those good ministers, who were believed to be good, turned out not to be good." It is fairly clear that Sima Qian was criticising King Huai of Chu. His historical conclusion is obvious, and he also felt sorry for those good ministers and talents who did not get fair treatment in their life.

Sima Qian's complaints are widespread in the *Shiji*. There are obvious examples in "The Biographies of the Wandering Knights" and "The Biographies of Usurers." In "The Biographies of the Wandering Knights" Sima Qian quoted from *Zhuangzi* that "those who steal hooks are killed while the men who steal kingdoms are ennobled. When such a person becomes a Prince, virtue and justice are on the side of the nobles." He commented, "This is not untrue." In "The Biographies of Usurers" Sima Qian used a proverb which says, "Sons of wealthy people won't have to be executed in the public market." He also commented, "These are not empty words." Just how angry was Sima Qian!

III Sarcastic Irony

The sarcasm of the *Shiji* is well known. The famous writer Lu Xun once said, "The life of sarcasm is the truth." After reading the *Shiji*, one might find Lu Xun's words perfectly correct. The *Shiji* contains a lot of factual reports, and with just a touch of explanation or a clue, the facts become ironically sarcastic. "The Biographies of Wan Shi and of Zhang Shu" is a good example. Shi Fen (also named Wan Shi) and four other family members all became high government officials, receiving salaries of 2,000 *dan* of grains, and they were called Nobleman of Ten-thousand-*dan*. Sima Qian described every detail of how cautious this family was and he praised their model behaviour. The whole biography was full of words of praise, yet the ugly hypocrisy of the family could easily be read between the lines, shown in his description of Shi Fen paying homage to the Emperor's horse. He would put on official clothing even at home when his children, who were lower level officials, came to visit. His pretentious acts were totally against human nature, and no one could possibly offer any genuine praise. Shi Jian, another figure in the biography, behaved similarly. When he became a secretary of the court, he would say things outside the court if he felt it right to do so, and sometimes he could make good points. However, when he was in the court, he acted as if he was someone who was not good at speaking. Emperor Wu favoured his behaviour and rewarded him handsomely. Under Sima Qian's dexterous pen, the great pretender Shi

但国破家亡的君主一个接一个，圣贤之君、昌盛之国几代都见不到。这是因为许多国君，他们认为的忠臣，其实并不忠，他们认为的贤臣，其实并不贤！很明显这里不单是批评楚怀王，而且是在总结历史的教训，为历史上许多忠臣、贤才鸣不平。

在《史记》中，司马迁的牢骚不平，随处可见。《游侠列传》、《货殖列传》都是较突出的例子。前者直接引用了《庄子》中的话"窃钩者诛，窃国者侯，侯之门，仁义存"（偷窃带钩的人要被杀，偷窃国家权柄的人却封了侯。他成了侯，也就会被称为有仁义的人）。并且评论说："非虚言也。"在《货殖列传》中引用谚语："千金之子，不死于市。"并也加以评论说："此非空言也"。这包含了多少辛酸和多大的愤慨啊！

（三）辛辣的讽刺

《史记》的讽刺艺术是有目共睹的。鲁迅说："讽刺的生命是真实。"读了《史记》，就更感到这句话的正确。《史记》所写多是事实，但一经作者暗示或点破，便成了绝妙的讽刺。如《万石张叔列传》写石奋一家五人都做到俸禄二千石的大官，号称万石君。列传中叙述这家人遵守行为规范而又孝顺谨慎。几乎满篇都是称颂的话，但从所描写的这家人的所作所为，却只能让人们感到他们的伪善卑劣。如石奋看到皇帝乘用的马匹，也要致敬，在家里见他做小吏的子孙也必定穿上朝服。矫揉做作，大背人情，实在不能赢得人们的赞美。书中描写石建，也写了不少他如何孝敬的话。可是，当他做了郎中令，估计避开别人，这事可以讲，他就大胆进言，讲得很中肯切实；但在朝会上，他却像是个不会讲话的。因此得到武帝欣赏，给予很高的待遇。这画龙点睛的一笔，就把石建伪装忠厚恭谨，其实世故狡诈的性格暴露无遗了。写石庆，司马迁先抓住了这样一

Jian's face was exposed to all. When writing about Shi Qing, Sima Qian captured one detail. When riding the imperial chariot, Shi Qing was asked by the emperor how many horses there were. He used his whip to count the horses one by one and then answered, "Six horses." He made himself so cautious and humble that he looked like an idiot. But, Shi Qing was considered the most casual among his brothers. he, however, became favoured by Emperor Wu and was able to keep the position of Prime Minister for a long time. How did such a person keep his office? By doing nothing, Sima Qian commented. For the nine years that he was in office, Shi Qing did not make any suggestions; he only tried to be very cautious. He was only a piece of furniture for display. Even though he was incompetent, Shi Qing tried to hold on to his position. When being scolded, he would not commit suicide nor resign. It happened that Emperor Wu needed a Prime Minister like him, and so he was able to keep his position till his death. Sima Qian's summing up for Shi Qing was that he hid his thoughts deeply within himself and behaved very cautiously. He made no good suggestions that would benefit the people. Sima Qian's comments negated all the praises listed previously and the readers easily understood the total sarcastic irony.

Sima Qian did not like any of the emperors of the Han Dynasty very much. The Emperor Gaozu and Emperor Wu were often the subjects of his sharp sarcastic irony. Liu Bang, the Emperor Gaozu who founded the Han Dynasty, did contribute a lot to history and he was a capable man. Even though he once became a local chief, he was not well-educated and had a lot of bad habits. Normally, historians would use the approach of "taking the higher moral ground and not paying attention to small details" and simply give a general description. Sima Qian was no normal historian. He respected the truth and left nothing out. Liu Bang indulged in wine and women, and he didn't pay his wine debts, boasting about himself in return for drinks and meals. And he looked down on scholars, even "urinating in their hats." He would also ride on the shoulders of a minister and asked, "What kind of an emperor am I?" Such descriptions might best describe the characteristics of a man. When describing Liu Bang, one thing could not be missed, that is, swearing, which is the characteristic that would describe Liu Bang best. When Liu Bang was stranded in Xingyang, Han Xin had an envoy sent over seeking to be installed as an acting prince. Upon hearing this, Liu Bang became furious and swore, "I am stranded here and hoping you were coming to rescue me. On the contrary, you bastard, you wanted to be a prince." Zhang Liang and Chen Ping kicked his leg and reminded him it was not a time to refuse Han Xin's request, and that it

个细节：石庆替皇帝赶车，皇帝问驾了几匹马，石庆用鞭子一一数过，才举手回答："六马。"谨慎如此，简直像个白痴了。然而石庆在石氏兄弟中还是最随便的!就是这样的人，却很能讨汉武帝的欢喜，长期担任丞相。他这个丞相怎么个当法呢？司马迁又加上冷冷的一笔：事情都不由丞相决定，丞相只是老实谨慎而已，在位九年，也没有提过正确的建议。——原来是聋子的耳朵，摆设而已。石庆虽无能，却很贪恋禄位，受到训斥，既不自杀也不去位。恰巧，大权独揽的汉武帝也很需要这样一个奴才丞相，所以他的位置竟十分稳固，任丞相一直到死。对这样一个人物，司马迁给他下了个总评语：石庆心思深藏不露，做事谨慎小心，但是并没有什么好主张能替百姓着想的。这便从最重要的方面推翻了前面的某些赞语，让人们切实地感到，通篇所写是事实也是讽刺。

司马迁对汉朝的皇帝是没有多少好感的，在他的笔下，汉高祖刘邦和汉武帝刘彻都是十分精彩的讽刺形象。刘邦这个汉朝的开国皇帝，在历史上是起了巨大作用的，并且也确有才干。可是他出身亭长，又缺乏文化教养，故而身上沾染了种种恶习。遇到这类情形，后来史书要为尊者讳，往往以"豁达大度，不护细行"两句，笼里笼统地交待完了。但司马迁却不，他尊重史实，将所搜集到的材料都组织了起来。于是刘邦如何好酒色，欠人酒账不还；如何说大话骗吃喝；如何轻视知识分子以至"溺儒冠"，如何骑在大臣脖子上问：我是什么样的皇帝。种种无赖行为都活灵活现地出现在人们眼前。《史记》写到刘邦讲话，往往离不开一个"骂"字，因为"骂"是最能体现刘邦性格特征的了。例如刘邦被围于荥阳，韩信偏偏派使者来，要求立为假王。刘邦大怒，骂曰：我被围困在这里，日夜都盼望你来帮我，你这混蛋，倒要自立为王！张良、陈平踢他的脚，提

would be wise to fulfill his request and do him a favour. Hearing this, Liu Bang changed his tone, but he went on swearing, "When a man pacifies a marquis, he could become a prince. Why the hell did he only want to be an acting prince? Coward!" The first swearing was due to anger. The latter one was something different. Swearing is not polite behaviour, and certainly not suitable for an emperor. However, this emperor was used to swearing. He was a witty emperor and could twist his thoughts quickly. His characteristics, such as wit, cunning, tolerance and jealousy, were all demonstrated in his swearing. Sima Qian did such a good job of describing him. Sui Jingchen, a playwright of the Yuan Dynasty, followed his descriptions and wrote a series of sarcastic plays on the *Emperor Gaozu's Return to His Hometown*.

Sima Qian not only criticised Emperor Wu in "The Treatise on the *FengShan* Ceremony" about his superstitious behaviours, he also wrote about it in other chapters. In "The Biography of Cavalry General Wei" and also in "The Biographies of Wan Shi and of Zhang Shu," the main figure was not Emperor Wu, but Sima Qian commented on him anyway. For example, Wei Qing took a suggestion from Ning Cheng and presented 500 pieces of gold to the parents of Madame Wang, who was most favoured by the Emperor. The Emperor, after learning this, "appointed Ning Cheng the Chief Commandant of Donghai." The flattering and the flattered could not escape the records of history. In "The Biographies of Wan Shi and of Zhang Shu," the Emperor despised the Prime Minister, who actually did nothing, but he could not sack him. He ordered the Prime Minister to retire from the court and then forbade him to resign. This greatly worried Shi Qing. The *Shiji* records the son of Heaven as exclaiming: "The national treasury is empty, the people destitute, and you want to send these people to the frontiers! You created such trouble and caused social unrest, and now you want to resign? Who do you want to blame all this on?" Obviously Emperor Wu wanted to make Shi Qing the scapegoat, and also wanted to keep his prime minister who did nothing but was obedient. Sima Qian's sarcastic intention was very obvious.

History records the truth and sarcasm is just one way of expressing the truth. In "The Biographies of Cruel Officials," Sima Qian often described those harsh officials who followed the Emperor's wishes and did all those unscrupulous things, and then he commented that, "the Emperor acknowledges his talent" or "the son of Heaven thinks him to be unselfish and that he has spared no efforts." These few words are the most sarcastic comments on Emperor Wu. There is another example in "The House of (Prime Minister) Xiao." When Liu Bang was leading an army, Xiao He stayed back in Guanzhong and

醒他这时并不可能禁止韩信称王，还不如卖个顺水人情。刘邦醒悟了，可他还是"骂"，不过骂的内容却完全变了样。他骂道：大丈夫平定诸侯，就是真王了，干吗还加个假字！真没出息。前者是怒骂，后者是鼓励的骂。骂是粗鲁无礼的行为，骂人是这位皇帝的习惯，但各种场合各种不同的骂法，却展现了刘邦机智、狡猾、宽容、忌刻种种性格特点或精神状态。《史记》所写刘邦的形象太生动了。所以元代散曲作者睢景臣即据其形象写了极富讽刺意味的《高祖还乡》套曲。

对于汉武帝刘彻，除了《封禅书》中对他的愚昧迷信作了讽刺性的描绘外，其他许多篇章也对他有所揭露、讽刺。如《卫将军骠骑列传》、《万石张叔列传》描写的主体并非汉武帝，但汉武帝却随处成了讽刺的对象。如卫青采纳宁乘的建议，以五百金献给武帝宠爱的王夫人的父母，武帝知道后，"乃拜宁乘为东海都尉"。拍马屁的与受拍的都逃不脱历史的鉴照。在《万石传》中，作者写了汉武帝对石庆这个挂名丞相既蔑视又不舍，他忽然命石庆告老回家，忽然又不许石庆辞职，弄得石庆惶惶不安，不知所从。书中记载，天子曰：仓库空虚，民众贫困流亡，你却主张将流民迁徙到边远地区，闹得动荡不安，闹出乱子，你倒要辞职，你想把责任推给谁啊？很明显，汉武帝需要石庆做替罪羊，需要这个只会顺从别无能耐的丞相。司马迁这样写，讽刺的意义是明显的。

历史的记载是真实的，讽刺艺术往往在于表达的方式。如《酷吏列传》常在叙述某些酷吏草菅人命，看皇帝眼色办事的种种劣行之后，轻轻加一句："天子闻之以为能"或"天子以为尽力无私"，这就构成了对汉武帝的绝妙讽刺。又如《萧相国世家》中，写刘邦在外作战，萧何留守关中，供应一切军需。但刘邦对他极不放心，经常派人监视。萧何为了免除刘邦的疑

was in charge of supplies. Liu Bang was suspicious of Xiao He and often sent his man to check on Xiao. In order to rid Liu Bang of his suspicion, Xiao He asked his soldiers to join the troops going to the frontier and used his own money to support the army. Furthermore, he purchased a great deal of land, and he also acted as a loan shark simply to damage his own reputation. On seeing all of this, Liu Bang became satisfied. It is repeatedly recorded that "the Emperor of the Han was happy," "the Gaozu Emperor was hilarious" and "His Majesty was very happy." Sima Qian did not provide many comments on these events, yet his words showed the relationship between the Prince and his subordinate and the vicious competition. Sima Qian had exposed the jealousy of Emperor Gaozu.

In the *Shiji*, Sima Qian vividly described the cold relationship between people in feudal society. Zhuo Wenjun, a widow, fell in love with Sima Xiangru and left her home. Zhuo Wangsun, Wenjun's father, was furious, and said, "Shame on my daughter, but how could I kill my own daughter? I will not give her a cent." Later on Sima Xiangru became a Zhong Lang and envoy to Xiyi. He went to Linqiong. Zhuo Wangsun, along with other celebrities in Ling Qiong, all tried to fawn on Sima Xiangru through his subordinates by offering cows and wine. Zhuo Wangsun sighed and said, "I should have let my daughter marry Sima the Supreme Minister." He then gave a lot of treasures to Wenjun, as much as he had given to his sons. Zhuo Wangsun's attitude changed totally, which reminded us of Butcher Hu in *The Scholars*. "The Biographies of the Marquis of Weiqi and of the Marquis of Wu'an" contains the best descriptions of the coldness of relationships. It describes all of the small things in daily life, for example, how Dou Ying, the Marquis of Weiqi who was no longer in power, was discarded by other people. He then went and curried favour with Tian Fen, the Marquis of Wu'an. A few years ago, the situation was totally different. The Biography also describes how the rebellious Guan Fu could not stand the way Tian Fen treated others and, having drunk too much wine, he lost his temper after a few drinks and scolded Tian Fen. In the end Guan Fu was killed, along with his whole family. It also shows how Dou Ying was killed by the intervention of Dowager Wang—Emperor Wu's mother. These conflicts so common in feudal society provided Sima Qian with material to illustrate the truth about feudal society and the relationships between people in that society. The most fabulous chapter must be the one when the Emperor ordered his ministers to discuss the rights and wrongs of Dou Ying and Tian Fen. The ministers in the court all knew that these two people had strong supporters, yet, they did not know Emperor Wu's intentions, so none of them wanted to say too

忌，一则派其子弟都去军前效力，再则悉以家私财佐军，三则多购买田地，放贷赚钱以贬低自己，表示不想得民心。这样果然每次都让刘邦放了心。传中一再说："汉王大悦"，"高帝乃大喜"，"上乃大悦"，相应地作出了反映。作者没有多说一句话，封建统治阶级内部勾心斗角、君臣间冷酷的利害关系不是昭然若揭吗？汉高祖忌刻的心理不是暴露在光天化日之下了吗？

司马迁对封建阶级人与人的关系，对封建社会的世态人情体验是很深刻的，在《史记》中有许多精彩的描写。如写死了丈夫的卓文君与司马相如相爱，离开了家庭，其父卓王孙"大怒曰：'女至不材，我不忍杀，不分一钱也'。"后来相如为中郎将奉使西夷，路过临邛。于是卓王孙和临邛的头面人物，都托司马相如的部属，献上牛、酒来巴结他。卓王孙叹息说：早就应该将女儿嫁给司马长卿了。并且分给女儿很多财物，与儿子相同。前后态度判若两人，很自然地使我们想起《儒林外史》中胡屠户的嘴脸。《史记》中刻画世态人情最淋漓尽致的要算《魏其武安侯列传》，全篇所写主要是日常生活中的事件。如：失势的旧贵族魏其侯窦婴怎样被趋炎附势之流所冷落，怎样降低身份去巴结新得势的武安侯田蚡——几年之间两人的地位倒了个个儿；那个强横好斗的灌夫又是怎样充当了一个打抱不平的脚色，在田蚡举行的宴会上使酒骂座，终被田蚡暗算，遭到灭族的惨祸；窦婴又怎样在汉武帝之母王太后的干预下被冤杀。这些封建阶级中经常存在的矛盾，到了司马迁的笔下，无不曲尽其妙，对世态人情的刻画无不具有深刻的讽刺意义。这篇文章最精彩的是武帝令群臣廷议魏其、武安的是非的一节。官僚们看到这两人都有强硬的后台，又摸不准武帝的意思，于是首鼠两端，回答得吞吞吐吐。搞得武帝也发了火，斥

much. Emperor Wu became furious and scolded Zheng Dangshi, "You had a lot to say about these two people. Now, when I asked you to comment on them in the court, you behaved like yoked horses. You all deserve to die." Emperor Wu had long hated Tian Fen because of his expansion of power. However, the Queen Dowager kept protecting Tian Fen as her half brother. Emperor Wu wanted to get rid of him, and he wanted his ministers to provide comments in the court so that he could use this to put pressure on his mother. Even though all ministers knew this, no one wanted to take any risks, which made the Emperor furious. After the Queen Dowager's intervention, Dou Ying was killed. At the end of the Biography, Sima Qian added his comments, that when Dou Ying and Tian Fen argued, Emperor Wu found Tian Fen at fault. It was because of the Queen Dowager that Dou Ying was killed. The denouncement in the court, and the performances of Emperor Wu and the Queen Dowager all added up to a wonderful sarcastic opera. One has to admire Sima Qian's mastery of words.

Ⅳ Full-fleshed characters

How is a writer able to convey the thoughts and characteristics of a real historic figure? How does a writer describe the complete character of a person? This was what the *Shiji* needed to tackle. Firstly, we see that Sima Qian was good at choosing stories that would reflect the characteristics of a person. Let's take "The Annals of Xiang Yu" as an example. Xiang Yu died when he was only 31 years old, yet he was a dominant figure at the transition from the Qin into the Han Dynasty. He participated in political struggles as well as battles. Sima Qian carefully chose three major events—the battle at Julu, the banquet at Hongmen and the ambush at Gaixia. Through the descriptions of these events Sima Qian gave his figure flesh and blood. The battle of Julu was a turning point for Xiang Yu, who understood that only by rescuing the State of Zhao could he escape the fate of being destroyed. He broke all cauldrons, sank his boats and made everyone determined to fight for victory, and at last he did win. The battle laid a solid foundation for Xiang Yu's position of Commander. Let's have a look at how Sima Qian told the story.

At that time, the number of the Chu soldiers outnumbered all others. Ten or more armies from different states had entrenched themselves outside Julu to rescue the city, but dared not take the field. When the Chu attacked the Qin, the others watched from their ramparts. None of the Chu soldiers failed to fight bravely. Their war-cries rent the

骂郑当时说：你平时讲魏其、武安的是非长短，头头是道，今天要你们在朝廷上讨论，倒像驾在车辕下的马驹一样局促不安。我要把你们一齐杀掉！原来这件事牵涉到宫廷内的矛盾，武帝早对田蚡揽权的行为心怀愤恨，但他母亲却竭力袒护她的这个同母异父弟弟，武帝让大臣们廷议也是为了对他母亲施加压力。可是大臣们心中有数，谁也不担这份风险，使得武帝大为失望。事情的结果是在太后大吵大闹一番之后，窦婴终于被杀。列传最后还补充说明：武帝在窦婴和田蚡闹矛盾时，是认为田蚡不对的，只是因为太后的缘故，才做了那样的判决。群臣的廷议，武帝、太后的种种表演，合起来不就是一幕生动的讽刺剧吗？今天读起来，真不能不佩服司马迁的艺术本领。

（四）完整的人物形象

写真人真事如何表现复杂的思想、性格？如何塑造完整的活生生的人物形象？这是《史记》需要解决的课题。首先我们看到，司马迁善于选择最能表现人物性格、最有故事性的题材。这里不妨以《项羽本纪》为例。项羽只活了三十一岁，但在秦楚之际却是个叱咤风云的人物，其一生主要事迹是政治、军事斗争。在这些事迹中，司马迁更集中笔墨，突出地描写了三件大事：巨鹿之战，鸿门宴，垓下之围。作者在这三个关键性段落中写活了项羽这个人物。巨鹿之战是扭转形势的一战。项羽明白只有救赵，才可避免被各个击破的命运，他"破釜沉舟"，作殊死战，终于取得胜利，这是很大的功绩，同时这一战役也奠定了项羽的统帅地位。司马迁有声有色地描写了这一战：

当是时，楚兵冠诸侯，诸侯军救巨鹿下者十余壁，莫敢纵兵，及楚击秦，诸将皆从壁上观，楚战士无不一

sky, striking terror into the hearts of all who heard them. None of the arms of Lords could disguise their fear. When the Qin was defeated, Xiang Yu summoned the other generals and they all fell to their knees after passing through the gate to Xiang Yu's camp and none dared look up.

From the contrast between the Chu army and the others, and by giving expression to thoughts, Sima Qian was able to bring to life the brave armies and even Xiang Yu's war-cries. The triple use of "none" was particularly evocative. The banquet at Hongmen was, again, a very critical moment for Xiang Yu. He was hesitant in deciding whether to kill Liu Bang or not, which revealed the complexity of his character. He was temperamental yet indecisive; he was sincere and fished for fame and honour; he was frank and direct. He loved to have brave soldiers, yet he did not know how to develop strategies. At the banquet, Xiang Yu was the dominant host, but he acted passively, because of his indecisiveness. By describing these two contrasting events, Sima Qian was able to outline Xiang Yu's strength and weakness. He did not simplify or give Xiang Yu only one mask with one expression. Sima Qian drew these historical figures from his observations of real life, and the figures were quite genuine. The third example was the event of Gaixia, where Xiang Yu totally lost his cause. He came to the end of his life, he sang, he bid farewell to his beloved concubine, and then he abandoned his excellent horse and committed suicide on the bank of Wujiang River. This event was described with such feelings of sadness. "The Annals of Xiang Yu" gave little description of how Xiang Yu had fought in the past, but Sima Qian did describe in detail Xiang Yu's battle before his death:

> Then with a mighty battle-cry, Xiang Yu charged. The Han troops scattered before him and he struck down one of their commanders. The Marquis of Chiquan, a cavalry commander, pursued Xiang Yu, who glared and bellowed at him so fiercely that the commander and his horse were so frightened that they fled for a few kilometers.

Xiang Yu, a hero who was able to lift up a heavy cauldron and was able to charge and fight with his army, came alive again under Sima Qian's pen. Exaggerated descriptions demonstrate Sima Qian's admiration and sympathy towards Xiang Yu. However, why such a hero lost so miserably is a question for all. Sima Qian answered that question. In the "Postface," Sima Qian criticized Xiang Yu severely. He said, Xiang Yu was overwhelmed by his achievements and adopted many wrong measures which led to his defeat, yet he claimed in the end that "Heaven is against me." It was utterly ridiculous for him to say so.

以当十，楚兵呼声动天，诸侯军无不人人惴恐。于是已破秦军，项羽召见诸侯将；入辕门，无不膝行而前，莫敢仰视。

　　从楚军与诸侯军的对照中，从诸侯将的心理、表情，简括有力地映衬出楚军的英勇和项羽的声威，而三个"无不"更把这种声威推到了极处。"鸿门宴"对项羽来说，又是一个关键时刻，围绕杀不杀刘邦的问题，展现了项羽多方面的复杂性格：他暴躁而又优柔寡断；他真诚而又沽名钓誉；他爽直但却轻率；他爱壮士却不知计谋。鸿门宴上，项羽是强大的一方，但却处处被动，这是和他性格上的这些特点分不开的。司马迁通过十分尖锐的戏剧冲突，刻画了一个既有优点也有缺点的活生生的项羽。司马迁绝没有将他的人物简单化、脸谱化，他的人物是从现实生活中提炼的，是十分真实的。第三个大事件垓下之围，是写项羽的覆灭。英雄末路，慷慨悲歌，别虞姬，弃骏马，最后自刎乌江。写得声情悲壮，**多姿多彩**。《本纪》全篇极少写项羽如何作战，在项羽行将灭亡之际，却对他的英勇善战，作了绘声绘色的描写：

　　　　于是项王大呼驰下，汉军皆披靡，遂斩汉一将。是时赤泉侯为骑将追项王，项王瞋（ chēn ）目而叱之，赤泉侯人马俱惊，辟易数里。

　　这一段写足了力能扛鼎，喑呜叱咤的项羽的英雄气概。夸张的笔墨反映了作者对项羽的钦佩与同情。然而不可一世的项羽，为何如此惨败，这是不能不引起人们深思的。对于这个问题，司马迁作了比较客观、公正的回答。在"太史公曰"的评语中，司马迁对项羽作了相当深刻的批判，指出：他被胜利冲昏头脑，采取了许多错误措施，却将自己最后失败归之于"天亡我也"，真是荒谬至极。历史人物的性格往往是丰富复杂的，

Historical figures may have complex characteristics and thoughts. It would be hard to judge their achievements and failures. Only a great writer like Sima Qian was able to show us such a colourful depiction of history through his book.

Also, in one event, there would be many historical figures. When writing a biography of each of the historical figures, it would be impossible to repeat the same stories in different biographies. Historical figures vary in their characteristics and they all need to be reflected in the biography. One clear guideline needs to be set, otherwise, the description would not be clear. Sima Qian created a style in writing which is called "compensating." Let's look again at the banquet of Hongmen. Guests at the banquet included Xiang Yu, Liu Bang, Zhang Liang and Fan Kuai. In the biography of each, it would be necessary to talk about that banquet. Sima Qian provided a full description in "The Annals of Xiang Yu." "The Annals of Emperor Gaozu" mainly explained the overall situation at that time, and described very little about the banquet. In "The House of Zhang Liang," Zhang Liang was described in his capacity as a strategist, and more focus was put on the meeting between Xiang Bo and Zhang Liang and Zhang Liang's implementation of his plan. The actual banquet was dismissed in one sentence, " ...later met Xiang Yu, as has been recorded in the account of Xiang Yu." "The Biography of Fan Kuai" did not deal with the first part of the banquet and focused on Fan's intervention, because this was the event that was connected with Fan and showed his contribution. Sima Qian pointed out that "On that day were it not for Fan Kuai, who charged into Xiang Yu's camp, Liu Bang's cause would have vanished." In this way, Sima Qian concentrated on each character's involvement in the one event and avoided any repetition. In "The Biography of Prince Wei," Sima Qian wanted to emphasise Prince Xinling's welcoming of all talents. In order to keep Xinling's good image he did not record incidents unfavourable to his characters. Those incidents such as Xinling did not dare to receive Wei Qi due to fear of Qin, and his limited understanding of Yu Qing, who dropped the position of the Minister in order to rescue Wei Qi and fled with Qi were put in "The Biographies of Fan Ju and of Cai Ze." By using the method of "compensating," Sima Qian maintained the completeness of each figure and by doing so, it also showed Sima Qian's love and resentment.

Thirdly, the *Shiji* used combined biographies to make the figures vivid with full characters. Sima Qian put people living in the same historical period and those who had close connections together and created combined biographies. Cases as such can been seen "The Biographies of Fan Ju and of Cai

其功过是非往往也有错综复杂的情况。也只有像司马迁这样的大作家，才能将历史的生动复杂的面貌再现出来。

其次，历史人物的事迹往往彼此相关，同一事件可以在不同传记中多次出现，这样便造成了重复，而对其中许多传记来说又显得累赘。历史人物的行为、性格往往是复杂的、矛盾的，传记既要有所反映，又要有一个基调，以免造成是非不清，爱憎莫辨的结果。为解决这一问题，司马迁发明了"互见法"。如鸿门宴的主要人物便有刘邦、项羽、张良、樊哙等，在以上四人的传记中，都有必要提到鸿门宴。司马迁便采取了详略互见的方法。《项羽本纪》最详，原因已如上述。《高祖本纪》只简单叙述了事实，侧重于当时形势，几乎不写宴会情形。《留侯世家》是从张良作为一个策略家的角度，详写了项伯见张良，张良用计的一段，关于宴会等等，只用"及见项羽后解"一句交待完毕。《樊哙传》则删去宴前种种，突出樊哙闯帐的事，因为此事才与樊哙有关，是樊哙的一件大功。作者还特别指出："是日微樊哙奔入营诮让项羽，沛公事几殆。"这样既避免重复又各得其所，是很巧妙的安排。又如《魏公子列传》，作者所要突出描写的是信陵君礼贤下士这一品格，故而关于信陵君因畏秦而不敢接待魏齐以及不了解为救魏齐而丢掉相位与之一起逃亡的虞卿，这些有损于这一品格的事，就不写在他本传中，而在《范雎蔡泽列传》中述及。在这里，司马迁便是用"互见法"，保持了人物性格的完整性，表现了作者鲜明的爱憎之情。

第三，《史记》为使其塑造的人物形象生动、完整，还采取了"合传"的办法。同时期的或者关系密切行为互相影响的人物，《史记》往往写成合传。如《范雎蔡泽列传》、《窦婴

Ze," and "The Biographies of Dou Ying, of Tian Fen and of Guan Fu." The methods Sima Qian applied to his work highlighted the themes and showed the contrasts among the figures. A further example is that of "The Biographies of Lian Po and of Lin Xiangru," the politicians of Warring States Period. At the beginning of the biographies, both Lian and Lin were mentioned and then two important events were described to bring the full light of the two figures. The first one was Lin Xiangru's bravery at the court of Qin, where he protected his country's dignity and safeguarded the jade of the He's family (*heshibi*), the priceless jade belonging to his country Zhao. The other story was how Lin again protected the dignity of his country at a diplomatic encounter in Mianchi. After these two events, Sima Qian wrote about the grudge between Lin and Lian caused by Lian's jealousy of Lin's popularity and described how Lian tried to obstruct and humiliate Lin, but Lin withdrew himself and tried every means to avoid confrontation with Lian. The first two events described at the beginning explained the reason for Lin's behaviour. Lin's explanation to his concession showed his magnanimity, and eventually ultimately moved Lian. Lin said:

> I was fearless and I scolded the King of Qin in his court and embarrassed his ministers. Why would I be afraid of General Lian? The Qin dared not to attack Zhao because of the existence of General Lian and me. We all know that when two tigers fight, one will be injured. And that would have been the case if we had fought. I do not confront General Lian because I put our country's fate before private feuds.

"I put our country's fate before private feuds." How well spoken! No wonder Lian heard it and he fastened a switch of thorns on his bare shoulders and sought forgiveness from Lin. The combined biographies emphasised the point that it was important for the general and the prime minister to have a good relationship and the common goal of fighting against their enemy. Lin Xiangru's virtue was manifested in his exemplary action of putting his country before himself. He acted fearlessly when he should and he withdrew himself when necessary. He won Sima Qian's great admiration.

Fourthly, various methods were used to describe the characteristics of each figure in the *Shiji*. For some, the most important events in their life were described; for others the chronological events of their lives were recorded. Sima Qian did not exclude any details that could demonstrate someone's character, but described each character fully. In "The Biography of Li Si," Sima Qian wrote about Li Si's comment on the difference between mice in a barn

田蚡灌夫列传》等。这样写有利于突出主题，表现人物性格。
《廉颇蔺相如列传》可为例证。这篇传记开头提到廉颇也提到
蔺相如，然后便突出地描写了蔺相如的完璧归赵和渑池斗争两
件大事，在秦廷和渑池会上，蔺相如的大智大勇被形象地刻画
出来了。然后再写到廉蔺的矛盾，原来老将廉颇不满意蔺相如
位在其上，便处处阻拦他、羞辱他，蔺相如却一再退让。有完
璧归赵和渑池会在先，蔺相如的一再退让决不是畏葸的表现便
有了充足的证据。因此，他对舍人所说的大义凛然的话才有了
着落，才深深地打动了廉颇。他说：

> 以秦王的威势，我敢在秦廷上当面叱责他，并且使
> 他的群臣难堪，我虽无能，怎么就单单惧怕廉将军呢！
> 我想强秦所以不敢攻打赵国是因为有我和廉将军两个人。
> 我们二虎相争必有死伤。我所以一再退让，是考虑到先
> 国家之急而后私仇啊！

"先国家之急而后私仇"，真是掷地作金石声的好语言，无
怪廉颇听说后，便负荆请罪了。很明显，这篇合传中所要突出
的正是将相和好，共同御侮的主题。蔺相如这一人物最具光彩
的，正是他为国家大计着想而不计个人得失的高尚风格。他当
勇则勇，当让则让，故而司马迁对其善处死生之际大为赞赏。

第四，《史记》塑造人物形象的方法是多种多样的。对有
的人物是选择其一生中最重要的事迹来写。有的人物则是从幼
年的事情直到生命的结束都有所交待。对于一些很能表现人物
性格的细节，司马迁是从不放过的。这些细节对于构成完整的
人物形象也确是不可少的。例如《李斯列传》开头便写了他
少年时看到仓中鼠和厕中鼠因居处不同待遇也大不一样，而发

and mice in a toilet. He said, "Humans are like mice, the major difference is their position." Li Si's view on life was fully reflected in the above-mentioned details. He went on and pursued his fame and wealth with his goals in mind. He contributed greatly to the unification of the states by the Qin. But he could not resist the temptation by Zhao Gao, who lured him and changed the will of the First Emperor of the Qin, and installed Hu Hai as the second emperor of the Qin. He later presented a letter of suggestion to Hu Hai and asked him to punish some ministers at will just to show his authority as an emperor. He couldn't have imagined that he was set up by Zhao Gao. He and his son were publicly executed. Before execution Li Si told his son, "I would like to take our yellow dog and go hunting for rabbits with you at the East Gate of Shangcai. How could we have times as such again?" This was Li Si's final words of repentance. Due to Li's case three families of his relatives were also executed. Li's other remark was "the pursuit of a higher position had led to the dead shackles locked on me." What Li Si had gone through was because of the philosophical thinking of his youth. The two comments made by Li truly demonstrated feudal bureaucrats' typical outlook on life and their journey of life. The phrase "Li Si and his yellow dog" became an idiom being frequently cited in Chinese poems. This is another example of the *Shiji's* summary power.

"The Biographies of Cruel Officials" contains more examples of the detailed descriptions of characters. Zhang Tang in the Han Dynasty was fond of detective work as early as in his childhood. Once, his father went out and asked the young Zhang to take care of the meat stored in house. Mice came out and ate the meat. On returning home his father blamed Zhang for not doing the job appropriately. Zhang Tang dug up the ground, found a mouse and a piece of the meat left. Zhang then acted as if he were dealing with a real criminal case. He prepared the indictment letter, presented exhibits, went through the interrogation and created proper case files. He then read out the sentence and executed the mouse immediatly. How extraordinary it was for a child to be interested in such detective work and processed it in such sophisticated procedure! It might have had something to do with what was happening in the society. In the Han Dynasty government paid great attention to official governance. That's the reason why a child had such knowledge. Cruelty had been cultivated early in Zhang Tang, who became the claws of the feudal emperor. Zhang Liang's encounter with Senior Huangshi is another example. When Zhang Liang was in Xiapi, he met a shabbily dressed old man on a bridge. When the old man came near Zhang Liang, he suddenly and deliberately dropped his shoes off the bridge. Looking at Zhang, the old man

出的感慨："人之贤不肖譬如鼠矣，在所自处耳。"这一细节表现了李斯的人生观。他一生追求功名利禄便是在这种人生观的指导下进行的。他曾为秦的统一作出了很大的贡献，但却经不住赵高的威胁利诱，同赵高一起违背秦始皇的遗诏，立胡亥为二世皇帝。为了阿顺胡亥，他又上督责之书，教胡亥任意处罚臣下，以显示皇帝的不测之威。谁知作茧自缚，遭到赵高的阴谋暗算，李斯及其次子同时被送上了刑场。死前，李斯回头对儿子说："吾欲与若（你）复牵黄犬，俱出上蔡东门，逐狡兔，其可得乎？"这又是一声慨叹！李斯竟被灭了三族。真是"因嫌纱帽小，致使枷锁扛"，李斯最后的结局，早在他少年时代便埋下了根子。两声慨叹前后呼应，这个封建官吏的生活道路是十分清晰的。司马迁写了这些细节，其意义尤在于揭示出颇为典型的封建官吏的人生观和生活道路。"东门黄犬"的典故，一再为后世诗文所引用，正说明了《史记》巨大的概括力量。

通过细节表现性格，我们还可以举出《酷吏列传》中张汤的例子。张汤幼年时便爱好判案，有一次老鼠偷吃了肉，张汤的父亲责怪他未将肉看好。张汤就挖开鼠洞，捉到老鼠，找到了咬剩的肉。于是就像真正升堂审案一样，有诉状、证物，又经过刑责，建立案卷，最后宣判，将老鼠当堂杀死。一个儿童，居然以考究判案为乐趣，而且如此老练，真是使人十分惊奇的事。这很可能与当时的社会风气有关。汉重吏治，儿童才会对判案有深刻的印象。而就张汤本人来说，则是从幼年起已酝酿着一种残忍的性格和成为封建帝王鹰犬的才能。再举出张良遇黄石公事，张良在下邳时，曾在桥上遇见一个穿着寒酸的老人。他走到张良旁边，忽然把鞋子故意掉到了桥下，看着张良说："小子！去把鞋取来！"张良一怔，简直想揍他一顿。但看他是个老人，忍下了，还给他取了鞋。老人又说："替我穿上！"

demanded, "Young man, go and get my shoes for me." Zhang Liang was in a shock and wanted to beat the old man up. But on second thoughts, he did not do it because of the old man's seniority. He went and picked up the shoes and gave them to the old man. The old man then said, "Put them on for me." Zhang Liang thought he might as well do a good deed, so he did put the shoes on the old man. The old man let him do his job and then smiled and walked on. Zhang Liang was aghast. The old man returned after a short while and said, "Young man, you are cut out for something big. Meet me here in the morning in five days' time." Zhang Liang agreed and went on the fifth day early in the morning. However, the old man was there already and he was not happy. He scolded Zhang Liang for being late for an appointment with a senior. He asked Zhang Liang to meet him even earlier in five days' time. Zhang Liang went only to find that he was late again. He was given another chance. This time he went at midnight and waited for the old man. The old man was happy and said it was what Zhang should do. He gave Zhang Liang a book, *On Military Arts by Jiang Taigong*. Zhang Liang later became successful because of this book. The reasons for Zhang Liang's success include his tolerance, honesty, politeness, and wisdom. These all contributed to his success later on.

Fifthly, to create a complete artistic image, the author's love and resentment must be expressed. There are many complicated figures in the *Shiji*. Even though they were all different, the author expressed his view very clearly, either of approval or disapproval, love or hatred. When the author wrote about those people he had been longing to meet, his passion was at the tip of his pen. Let's take the example of his description of Prince Xinling. During the rule of Emperor Wu the central power of the imperial court was strengthened. He also regarded Confucianism as the orthodox state ideology. Many people belonging to other schools could never have any chance of putting their talents to use. People with military skills had no opportunities to demonstrate their abilities. Scholars became companions at tours and banquets. Many of them were not happy about the situation. In their view, during the Warring States Period, the "hundred schools of thought" saw the importance of "protégés" who contributed greatly to society. Those periods were the best times for protégés. Dongfang Shuo explained his view on this extremely thoroughly in his article "Answers to Questions." Sima Qian had been suppressed and looked down upon, and he was not happy with his status, either. When he wrote about Prince Xinling, who lived in the Warring States Period, and cared about protégés irrespective of their social status, Sima Qian could not hold back his feelings. The best description was about Prince Xinling's welcoming of Hou Ying, the

张良想：好事做到底吧，就恭恭敬敬地给他穿上了。老人也不客气，伸着脚由他穿上，笑着走了。张良很惊讶，目送他走去。老人走了不远又折回，说你这小子可教！过五天，一大早，与我在此会见。张良答应了，五天后，一早，张良到了那里，老人已先到了。发怒说，与老人约会，为什么来晚了。再过五天早点来。张良更早去，还是晚了。又过五天，不到半夜就去了，过了一会儿，老人才到，这回老人高兴了，说应当这样，然后就传授给张良一册《太公兵法》，张良因此取得成功。这件事表现了张良忍耐、诚信的品格，并且懂礼貌、有智慧，这都是张良日后取得成就的基础。

第五，塑造一个完整的艺术形象，作者的爱憎分明是一个不可缺少的条件。《史记》中的人物，尽管复杂多样，但作者的基本态度是肯定还是否定，是同情还是憎恶，是赞美还是批判总是十分清楚的。尤其写他"心向往之"的人物，更是笔端凝聚着感情。如对信陵君的描写就是如此。汉武帝时中央集权加强，独尊儒术，诸子百家无所展其长，策略之士无所逞其技。文学之士只起陪侍游宴的作用。不少作者对这样的地位是很不满的。在他们的心目中，战国时代百家争鸣，各国重"士"成风，"士"也确实发挥了很大作用，那真可说是"士"的黄金时代。这意思以东方朔的《答客难》讲得最为透底。司马迁对所处被压抑受轻视的地位也是不满的，所以在记叙战国时以礼贤下士闻名的信陵公子时，便不免赞美之情溢于言表了。其中

warden of the east gate of the city:

> The Prince then prepared a banquet to entertain the guests. When all had arrived and were seated, the Prince took a carriage and left the seat of honour empty for Hou Ying. He then went to collect Hou Ying in person. Hou Ying, dusting his tattered clothes and cap, got onboard. He took the honourable seat without a word of politeness, just to see how the Prince would react. The Prince, with reins in hand, appeared even more respectful. Hou later said to the Prince, "I have a friend who is in the market. Please take me there." The Prince then took the carriage there and waited while Hou talked to his friend Zhu Hai. Hou talked for a long while and watched the Prince who showed no sign of impatience. While the guests at the banquet, the generals, ministers, noblemen and protégés were waiting for the Prince to start the feast, people at the market place all saw the Prince driving the carriage for Hou Ying. All his other guests were cursing Hou Ying, who, seeing the Prince did not change his demeanour at all, bade farewell to his friend and boarded the carriage. When they arrived, the Prince made Hou Ying take the seat of honour and introduced him to all his guests. All were amazed.

It was quite an unusual scene for a well known prince to have welcomed an unknown elderly gate-keeper. Sima Qian retold the whole event by describing the actions of Prince Xinling and Hou Ying, their expressions and the behaviour of the onlookers. It is as good as the famous three visits to Kong Ming as described in *The Stories of the Three Kingdoms*. It was pointed out that in "The Biography of Prince Xinling," the word "Prince" was used 147 times to address Xinling and it did not sound repetitive. In the above-quoted text alone it appeared 13 times. It seemed as if Sima Qian was a great photographer who set his camera on the Prince and we could see each and every bit of his excellent performance. Sima Qian also demonstrated his great admiration for the Prince.

It was because of his passion that Sima Qian was able to let the people in his book live forever.

V Splendid Language

The literary achievements of the *Shiji* mainly come from the splendid language used in it.

The *Shiji* employs the speech patterns of individuals to showcase personality. For example, when seeing the First Emperor of the Qin's

最精彩的是信陵君亲自迎接夷门监者侯赢的一段：

> 公子于是乃置酒，大会宾客。坐定，公子从车骑，虚左，自迎夷门侯生。侯生摄敝衣冠，直上载公子上坐，不让，欲以观公子。公子执辔愈恭。侯生又谓公子曰："臣有客在市屠中，愿枉车骑过之"。公子引车入市。侯生下见其客朱亥，俾倪，故久立与其客语，微察公子。公子颜色愈和。当是时，魏将相宗室宾客满堂，待公子举酒；市人皆观公子执辔；从骑皆窃骂侯生；侯生视公子色终不变，乃谢客就车。至家，公子引侯生坐上座，遍赞宾客。宾客皆惊。

一个著名的贵族公子这样谦恭地迎接一个不知名的看守城门的老头，实在是很难得的事。司马迁从信陵君与侯生各自的动作、表情，周围人们的种种反应，生动曲折地描写了这件事的过程，和《三国演义》中的三顾茅庐几乎有异曲同工之妙。前人早已指出《魏公子列传》中，作者用了一百四十七个"公子"来称呼信陵君，却并不显得重复，就如上面所引一小节，"公子"已出现了十三次。可是就好像特写镜头一再对准了主角一样，每次称"公子"都让我们看到他卓越的表演，并且也从中体现出作者无比倾慕、赞颂之情。

作者爱憎鲜明，才有可能赋予其所塑造的形象以长久的生命力。

（五）生动的语言

《史记》文学的成就，多半得力于生动的语言。

《史记》人物的语言是力求其个性化的。比如同样看到秦始皇出巡的排场，捣乱的项羽道："彼可取而代也！"没出息的刘邦却说："大丈夫不当如是耶？"这意思相同，表达却不

procession, Xiang Yu said, "I can replace him!" While Liu Bang said, "Shouldn't a great man be like that?" The intention of the two were the same, but they expressed their desires in different ways. The personalities of each could be seen from the language they used. Xiang Yu was the grandson of Xiang Yan, a known general of the Chu Dynasty. Born into a noble family, he was bold and unconstrained. When he saw the procession he was able to make the "bold comments." On the contrary, Liu Bang had been a commoner before becoming a junior official in the feudal system. When he saw the procession of the First Emperor of the Qin, all he could do was to admire. He did not have the courage to "replace him." However, it was his aspiration that kept him going and made him a great man. He was able to reflect upon himself and kept improving himself.

Another example is "The House of Chen She." Chen She's companion who farmed with him when they were young visited Chen's palace and commented, "Hay, mate, you are now a king and you are glorious." Such language was used by uneducated labourers. The labourer who farmed with Chen She did not imagine this could happen. When he actually saw what had happened, it was natural for him to voice his surprise. He was simple and he thought he could use the casual language such as "hay, mate" in the same way as when he farmed with Chen She. Sima Qian put these words in the *Shiji* not for the collection of rare comments, but to show a very important historical fact. After the farmer had said that, he was laughed at and later on was blamed for causing King Chen She to lose face. The farmer's further elaboration on Chen She's poverty in the past gave reasons for people around Chen to slander him. Chen thus killed him, the old friend from childhood. Chen She forgot his past. All those who had shared earlier difficulties with him left him. Only the calculative mean people were left around Chen She. Sima Qian clearly pointed out that this was the reason for Chen She's ultimate failure. The use of individual speech helped achieve Sima Qian's point. Another similar example is "The Biography of Prime Minister Zhang." The Emperor Gaozu of the Han planned to abolish Crown Prince Liu Ying and give the title to Ru Yi, the Lord of Zhao. Zhou Chang, the Chief Imperial Censor argued strongly in the court against this. Zhou Chang, according to "The Biography of Prime Minister Zhang," stuttered. He was furious at the time and he said, "I cannot speak well, but I, I understand it is inappropriate. Your Majesty wants to abolish the Crown Prince, and I, I do not want to obey the edict." The mimicking of Zhou Chang's stuttering was not for amusement, but was intended to faithfully depict the person. When we read these, we could almost hear Zhou and feel the

一样的两句话，极生动地表现了两个人不同的性格和心理。项羽是楚国将军项燕的后代，出身高贵，豪爽粗放，他看到秦始皇车驾，冲口而出便说了那么一句"豪言壮语"。而刘邦则是出身平民，作为一个封建统治基层的小官吏，见到秦始皇的车驾，他是艳羡的，但却没有勇气去"取而代之"。然而，他又是个"胸怀大志"的人，很想爬上高层的地位。这种种原因就使他只可能用一个反躬自问的句子，来表达他无限向往之情。

又如《陈涉世家》，写到陈涉当年佣耕时的同伴，看到陈涉的宫殿陈设发出这样的赞叹："伙颐！涉之为王沈沈者。"这是当时地道的口语，用今天的话就是说："好家伙！陈涉当上了王爷可真阔气啊！"这样的话当然是切合一个没有文化的劳动者的身份的。此人当年与陈涉一起佣耕的时候，曾不相信像他们这样的人还能富贵。所以当他看到陈涉真的富贵了，自然会发出惊叹。这简单的一句口语，表现了此人的朴实单纯，他还像当年一样，讲起话来一无顾忌。司马迁把这句话写进《史记》并不是为了猎奇，而是为了形象地说明一个重要的历史事实。这个佣耕者，说了"伙颐"一词被当时传为笑谈，大有损于陈涉"王者的体面"，加之他又毫无顾虑地大讲陈涉贫困时的情形。陈涉周围的小人便挑动陈涉杀了这位故人。陈涉忘记了过去，从前共患难的朋友都离开了他。他身边只剩下一些卑鄙小人。司马迁正确地指出这也是陈涉失败的重要原因。这句个性化的口语，在说明这一情况时，确实起了重要的作用。与此相类，《张丞相列传》中，写汉高祖要废太子立赵王如意，御史大夫周昌在朝廷上竭力争辩的事。列传中交待周昌有口吃的毛病，又盛怒，争辩说："臣口不能言，然臣期期知其不可，陛下虽欲废太子，臣期期不奉诏。"摹写周昌口吃也并不是为了逗趣，而是使读者如见其人，如闻其声，更深地感受到周昌

uprightness of him. This description reminds us of Shi Xiangyun in another very known novel *The Dream of the Red Chambers*. Shi was someone whose pronunciation was not clear sometimes, but she was well known for being a straight character. The way she spoke was associated with her character. The same applies to Zhou Chang. Sima Qian was good at bringing characters to life through their own words. Sima Qian, when describing Wang Wenshu, a harsh official, wrote, "Wang stamped his foot and said, 'Pity! I wish that the winter could be one month longer so it could give me time to finish all my tasks of execution!' " In that time it was forbidden to execute in spring. One sentence is enough to explain how cruel this harsh official was and how much he wanted to kill.

The *Shiji* also describes the expressions which show people's feelings. Stories in "The Biography of Prince Pingyuan" (named Zhao Sheng) is a good example. Prince Pingyuan planned to lobby the State of Chu to form an alliance to fight the State of Qin. He needed to take 20 talented followers amongst the protégés, in his house. He had chosen 19 and needed one more. Mao Sui, one of his protégés came up to offer himself. Prince Pingyuan asked Mao how many years he had been in his house. Mao Sui responded, "Three years." The Prince went on and said, able men were like spears in a bag. They would poke out. Mao had been in his house for three years and he had heard no comments about Mao. He went on and said, "Sir, you do not perform well. Sir, you are not able. Sir, you may not go." The Prince spoke with curt finality and used the word "sir" three times from which we can see he was disdainful of Mao Sui. Later on Mao Sui was able to persuade the Prince to let him go along. When talking to the King of Chu who was very hesitant about fighting Qin, Mao Sui went to the court wearing his sword. He talked and coerced the King, and finally achieved an alliance agreement. Mao Sui came home with great achievements. Prince Pingyuan said, "I don't think I should judge anyone any more. I have seen hundreds of men, if not a thousand, and I thought I was able to judge their talents. But about Mao, I was wrong. Mao's presence in Chu made our country more important than the *Jiuding* and the *Dalü* ❶ . Mao used his eloquent tongue and achieved more than what could be done with tens and thousands of soldiers. I should not judge anyone any more."
Prince Pingyuan's sincere confession and the mention of Mao Sui three

坚忍质直的性格。这使我们联想到《红楼梦》中所写史湘云说话咬字不清的特点，这个特点竟和史湘云娇憨爽直的性格密不可分了。用人物的一句话，生动地表现出人物的性格、心理，真是司马迁极大的本领。如他写酷吏王温舒在春回大地之际，"顿足叹曰：'嗟乎！令冬月益展一月，足吾事矣！'"（当时规定春天不行刑），不用再多说一句话，这个残忍好杀的酷吏，已经活生生地站在人们眼前了。

表现性格之外，《史记》的语言还极富表情，能够很生动地传达人物当时的情感。例如《平原君列传》记平原君赵胜去楚国约合纵抗秦，准备带门下食客二十人同去。已选了十九人，门下客毛遂自荐。平原君问毛遂在此几年了，毛遂回答三年。平原君说，贤能之士在世上，就好像铁锥装在袋子里，尖头立刻会露出来，现在先生已在我的门下三年了，周围的人没有谁赞扬过你，我也从来没有听到过，"是先生无所有也。先生不能。先生留。"结末三句话斩钉截铁，连称"先生"，含有轻视的意味。后来毛遂说服平原君，还是跟着去了。会谈中，楚王犹豫，不肯合纵，毛遂按剑上殿，连说服带威胁，终于订立了合纵的盟誓。毛遂立了大功，回赵之后平原君说："我不敢再来评定士人了！我评定士人多着说上千人，少着说也上百，自以为不会错过天下之士，可是今天对于毛先生却错过了！毛先生一到楚国，就使得赵国显得比九鼎、大吕❶都更有份量！毛先生用他的三寸之舌胜过了百万之师！我真是不敢再来评定士人了！"这真是俗话说的："有眼不识泰山。"司马迁摹写平原

---

❶ 译者注：九鼎，传说为夏朝大禹所铸，鼎是国家权力的象征。大吕是大钟的名称，为周朝的国宝。

❶ Translators' notes: *Jiuding*, the "Nine Tripod Cauldrons" were created by Yu the Great in the Xia Dynasty. It is used to symbolise the power of nations. The *Dalü* was the Great Bell, the national treasure of the Zhou Dynasty.

times showed his respect for Mao, which is in such contrast to what he had said before going to the State of Chu. He repeated, "I should not judge anyone any more," which strengthens the contrast.

The repetitive use of a word, or a sentence, will also emphasise the feelings of a person. Examples can be found in "The House of Chen She." Chen She and the other nine hundred poor labours were recruited for army. They could not reach the frontier on time due to the heavy rain. All were facing death penalty. Before rising in revolt, Chen She discussed his plan with Wu Guang. "We will definitely die because we are late. We would also die if we rise in arms. As we would all die anyway, why don't we die for our country?" He said similar things to encourage soldiers to join him. He said, "Now we've encountered this heavy rain and we will all miss our deadline. The punishment of missing the deadline is execution. Even if we arrived at the frontier and could be freed from execution, sixty or seventy percent of men who serve at the front will die. Strong men should die with fame and honour. There are no born kings, noblemen, generals and ministers." In the first text, "die" was mentioned four times. In the latter one, "execution" was mentioned twice. The emphasis made the desperate situation very clear to the conscripts. They needed to rise and seek an opportunity to live. The use of "die" pointed out the nature of the revolt, that is, they were forced to do so and they must undertake extreme danger. The comparison of different types of death made the revolt legitimate. They were faced with death, no matter what they did. If they were to take their chances and revolt, they could have an opportunity to live. "There are no born kings, noblemen, generals and ministers" is another sentence of encouragement full of confidence.

The *Shiji* often contains expressions of feelings. Sometimes, when adding descriptions of actions, it presents more vivid scene to the readers. In "The Biographies of Fan Ju and of Cai Ze," Fan Ju, hid himself in a carriage of Wang Ji and escaped to the State of Qin. On the way, the carriage met with Marquis Rang, a powerful minister in Qin. Marquis Rang checked to see if any protégés of other Lord had come along. Wang Ji lied to him, saying that there weren't any. Fan Ju, after Marquis Rang left, said, "I heard Marquis Rang was a smart person but slow on the uptake. He even suspected that there was someone in the carriage but he forgot to check it." Saying this, Fan Ju hurriedly got off the carriage and said, "He would regret this." We can see vividly the hasty manner in which Fan Ju left.

The *Shiji* using descriptive language provided the readers with impressive and detailed images of what was happening. In "The Houses of the Empress'

君自我检讨，不胜慨叹的口气，前后呼应"胜不敢复相士"，一段话中三称"毛先生"，不胜钦佩恭敬之至。与前一段话相比较，同样连称先生，但所传达的人物的感情多么不同，又多么生动！

用重复的词、句来表达人物的感情，在《陈涉世家》中也可找到很好的例子。陈涉在起义之前曾与吴广商议："今亡亦死，举大计亦死；等死，死国可乎！"后来在鼓动戍卒参加起义时，他们也说了意思相同的一段话。他们说："公等遇雨，皆已失期。失期，当斩。藉弟令毋斩，而戍死者固十六七。且壮士不死即已，死即举大名耳，王侯将相宁有种乎！"前一段话接连用了四个"死"字，后一段话连用了两个"斩"字，三个"死"字，把当时迫急的形势，人物铤而走险、死中求生的心情，活脱脱地表现了出来。连用"死"字，说明了农民起义实在是"逼上梁山"，担着极大的风险。而几种"死"的比较，又把农民起义的正义性凸现了出来。同样是死，那么，被虐待而死，逃亡而死，或引颈受戮，都远不如为国事而死，举大计而死，何况发动起义便有生的可能。"王侯将相宁有种乎！"是一句号召鼓动的话，也是一句充满胜利信心的话。

表情语言，在《史记》中是用得很多的，有时结合动作，则更能传达当时的情景。如《范雎蔡泽列传》写范雎藏在王稽车中逃亡到秦国，路遇秦国权臣穰侯。穰侯查问有没有诸侯的门客同来，王稽骗他说没有。穰侯走后，"范雎曰：'吾闻穰侯智士也，其见事迟。乡者疑车中有人，忘索之。'于是范雎下车走曰：'此必悔之！'"一句话没有说完便下了车，边走边说，综观全句话，充分表现了范雎匆忙的状态、惶急的心情。

《史记》的语言在描写事态时，很有表现力，我们可以举《外戚世家》记窦皇后与其弟窦广国相见的事为例。窦皇后原

Relatives," the meeting between Empress Dou and her brother Dou Guangguo was an extraordinary example. Empress Dou, before becoming the Empress, was a maid in the imperial palace. When she was sent to Daidi, she sadly bade farewell to her little brother in an inn. Dou Guangguo had been living in poverty. He later came to find his sister who was now the Empress. However they had been separated for years and it was hard to prove Guangguo was the Empress' brother. Guangguo then retold the scene when he had parted with his sister. On this, Sima Qian wrote, Emperor Wen also inquired into this. And he found the descriptions were similar and asked if Guangguo had any further evidence. Guangguo said, "Before my sister went westbound, she came to say goodbye. Before departure she begged for some water to wash my hair. She also asked for food for me." The Empress tried to hold back her tears but couldn't. She burst into tears, and all the servants knelt on the ground and cried to add to the Empress' sadness." Lin Shu wrote an article "The Disquisitions Written in Chunjue Study" and commented on Sima Qian's description of the departure. He said that Lady Dou knew she would not have any chance of meeting her young brother again, and their meeting at the inn would be very brief. Although seeing her brother looked like a beggar with dirty face and hair and was very hungry, all she could do was to beg for water and some food for him, just to fulfill her duty as an elder sister. In a short time she had to leave and would have no ability to help her younger brother. Lin Shu said, "Sima Qian used just a few words and readers are able to see the sad departure" and that "the Grand Historian wrote with true passion indeed." The use of the words "begged" and "asked for" was enough to illustrate to readers the sad departure between a helpless maid and her helpless young brother. The love between these two siblings was contained in Sima Qian's few words. No wonder Empress Dou burst into tears when she was reminded of this departure. Sima Qian, at this time, did not forget Lady Dou was then the Empress, and added that "all the servants knelt on the ground and cried to add to the Empress' sadness." How could the servants have added to the sadness? When they saw the Empress was crying, how could they be ignorant and not do anything? They had to pretend to cry. The word " add" showed Sima Qian's humour.

The descriptive language in the *Shiji* is also colourful. Liang Qichao, the famous Chinese scholar and reformist during the Qing Dynasty, once said, "The *Shiji* explains very clearly some complicated events, for example, 'The Biographies of Usurers,' 'The Biographies of the Xiongnu' and 'The Biographies of the Southwest Barbarous People.' The life-stories are told with clarity, which

是宫女，被驱迫去往代地时，曾与其幼弟广国在传舍中诀别。后来窦广国来认他的成了皇后的阿姊，分手多年，已互不相识，广国乃举出分别时的情景以为验证。关于这件事，司马迁写道：文帝召见询问，事情经过不差，又问他有什么可以证明。广国说："姐西去时，和我在传舍中诀别，讨了一些水替我洗头，又要了点饭给我吃，然后才走。""于是窦后持之而泣，泣涕交横下，侍御左右皆伏地泣，助皇后悲哀。"关于这一段描写，林纾在《春觉斋论文》中有很好的分析。大意是说，窦姬深知这一去再无相见之期，在旅舍中与幼弟相会也只有片刻时间，看到弟弟蓬首垢面，饥饿难忍也只能最后尽一尽姊姊的心意，一个"丐"字一个"请"字，正说明"不丐且不得沐，不请且不得食"，沐后饭后，匆匆登车，再无法顾及弟弟的下落了。林纾赞美司马迁"寥寥数语，而惨状悲怀，已尽呈纸上"。"史公之写物情，挚矣。"一点不错，"丐"、"请"二字包含了多少辛酸。没有人身自由的宫女和无依无靠的弱弟被迫分离时的惨痛，那"相呴以湿，相濡以沫"的手足之情，全包含在这寥寥数语之中了。无怪窦皇后忆起当日情景，也不免涕泪交流。然而，司马迁并没有忽略昔日的窦姬如今已是皇后了。于是加上了"侍御左右皆伏地泣，助皇后悲哀"这样一句。悲哀而可相助，闻所未闻！侍御左右本无多大哀感，但皇后如此痛哭流涕，怎么能冷眼旁观呢？于是也要做出哭的样子。这个"助"字实在幽默、风趣，有着十分丰富的内涵。

《史记》的叙述语言也很精彩。梁启超说："极复杂之事项——例如《货殖列传》、《匈奴列传》、《西南夷列传》等所叙，皆能剖析条理，缜密而清晰，其才力固自绝。"《史记》长篇叙事多用提振之词，如"是时"、"当是时"或"其三年"、"其明

contributed to the *Shiji*'s integrity." In the *Shiji*, the passage of time was made clear by the use of such phrases as, "at that time," "at which time," "for three years," "the next year," "the winter" and even "more than one hundred years afterward." These words made the time line very clear. When writing about geographic scenes, Sima Qian paid much attention to the location and direction of events. Gu Yanwu said, "During the Qin and Han dynasties the movements of the army and the routes they took were very complicated. Only the Grand Historian knew exactly where each battle took place. If he were to name the places, it would not be easy for readers. But by using the direction words such as east, west, south or north for the movements and locations in the stories, he made it easy for readers to follow. " Sima Qian was able to tell the events so clearly, which was much due to his personal visits and investigations to many places.

Pre-Qin histories in the *Shiji* were mainly based on historical facts on books such as *The Book of History, The Annals Compiled by Zuo, The History of Different States* and *The Records of the Warring States*. How to make use of these existing materials was another issue that Sima Qian had to tackle. For those well preserved records, Sima Qian only amended a few words; for materials either incomplete or having a lot of new information, he would rewrite them with artistic touches; for materials written in ancient text that people could not understand, he would often translate them into the commonly used language or provide explanations. For example, he changed "Qin Ruo Hao Tian" in *The Book of History* to the plain language of "Jing Shun Hao Tian" (to respect the Heaven); also "Shu Ji Xian Xi" to "Zhong Gong Jie Xing" (to encourage all works); and that "Zai Cai Cai" to "Shi Shi Shi" (to start the work). We know that when writing the *Shiji*, Sima Qian wanted to "keep his book in the famous mountain and to share it with the people who have the same interest as his." He did not want to produce an unfathomable work that would be difficult for readers to understand and scare them off. That is why he only used simple language. Could we take it as Sima Qian's care for readers?

The poetic language of the *Shiji* can also be seen in the use of run-on sentences, repeated sentences and repeated words which made the language powerful. In "The Biography of Qu Yuan and of Jia Yi," Sima Qian wrote, "Qu Yuan hated the fact that the King was unwise, that brightness was being blocked by slanderous words, that the public interest was being destroyed by evil, and that uprightness being replaced by wrongdoing. It is because of the big worries and deep thinking that Qu Yuan wrote the great poem 'The Lament.' "

年”、“其冬”一直到“其后百有余年”，交代时间有条不紊。叙述中有交代，有呼应，或用省笔，或用伏笔，总是有起有落，头头是道。其叙述地理形势，则很重视方位。顾炎武说：“秦楚之际，兵所出入之涂，曲折变化，唯太史公序之如指掌。以山川郡国不易明，故曰东、曰西、曰南、曰北，一言之下，而形势了然。”能叙述得如此清楚，当然跟司马迁作过许多实际调查是分不开的。

《史记》写秦以前史，主要根据《尚书》、《左传》、《国语》、《战国策》等书。对这些现成资料如何运用，司马迁是采取了各种不同方法的。有的材料本身较完备，他只作了字句的改动，有的材料不全或收集到较多的新材料，他便加以改写，作较大的艺术加工。而对于语言古奥难懂的古书，他引用时往往径直翻译成汉代通用语，或增加解释性的说明。例如《尚书》中的“钦若昊天”他便改写为“敬顺昊天”；“庶绩咸熙”他改作“众功皆兴”；“载采采”改作“始事事”。我们知道司马迁写作《史记》是要“藏之名山，传诸其人”的，但他一点也不想写得高深莫测，让读者望而生畏，却处处为当时的读者着想，竭力写得通俗易懂一些。这也可算司马迁民主性的表现吧！

《史记》的叙述语言往往很有抒情性。他用排句、叠句、叠字等等形式，使语句有很大的动人力量。如《屈贾列传》叙述屈原写作《离骚》，说：“屈平疾王听之不聪也，谗谄之蔽明

From these descriptions we learn about Qu Yuan's anger about the darkness of the State of Chu at the time. It was the overflowing of these suppressed feelings that caused Qu Yuan to write " The Lament." How poetic were Sima Qian's words!

也，邪曲之害公也，方正之不容也，故忧愁幽思，而作《离骚》。"一连串排比的句子使我们感到屈原忧愤之深之大，楚国政治之黑暗，之不平。压抑既久，喷薄而出，才写作了《离骚》。这样的语句，真可说是诗的语言了。

汉代文物，著名的"长信宫灯"
Cultural Relic of the Han Dynasty, the Famous Changxin Palace Lantern

毛遂提剑威胁楚王，终于订立了盟约
Mao Sui Coerced the King of Chu Wearing His Sword and Finally
Achieved an Alliance Agreement

In the *Outline of Literature of the Han Dynasty*, Lu Xun said, the *Shiji* is the "pinnacle of all historians, and it is like the great poem 'The Lament' without rhymes." This is high praise indeed for the *Shiji*.

From the perspective of historical records, the *Shiji* is highly successful. It is wide-ranging in its coverage, making significant contributions to subjects such as astrology, geography, philosophy, military events and literature. The *Shiji* continued the great tradition of Chinese historians of "no boasting and no covering up," and it served as a good example for historians who came after Sima Qian. Zheng Qiao, a historian of the Song Dynasty, once said, "No historians could change his methods; no scholars could abandon his book." Zhao Yi, a historian of the Qing Dynasty, also commented that it was "the ultimate guide for historians." It goes without saying that they all commented on the style of the *Shiji*, although they did not delve deeply into the spiritual meanings of the *Shiji*. Sima Qian's ambition was to "examine all that concerns Heaven and man, penetrate the changes of the past and present, and complete a work of my own." Also, his aspiration to "observe the history of each dynasty at its beginning and tell the end" and to "see the peak of a dynasty and know the fall" exceeded that of any other historians in the Chinese feudal society. After the *Shiji* came into being, many historians tried to copy the style and wanted to continue the book. However, "many history books were of inferior quality and could not be considered sequels to the *Shiji*" and the records were lost. In the Eastern Han Period, Ban Biao followed the style of the *Shiji* and wrote 65 chapters to be attached to the *Shiji*. Ban Biao's example was a foundation for his son Ban Gu to write *The Chronicles of the Han Dynasty*. After the *Shiji*, *The Chronicles of the Han Dynasty* is a very influential book. It followed the style of the *Shiji*, and put the feudal houses into biographies and changed Treatises to Logs (*Zhi*). *The Chronicles of the Han Dynasty* is a book covering only one dynasty, the Western Han Dynasty. Historical records before Emperor Wu rely on the *Shiji*. However, Ban Gu was a conservative man. Even though *The Chronicles of the Han Dynasty* was not as great a work as the *Shiji*, it used similar sentence patterns. Due to the fact that the government at the time encouraged the *Pianti* Style of essays, the influence of *The Chronicles of the Han Dynasty* became greater than the *Shiji* for a long period of time. "Some famous scholars of the Han and Jin periods did not even know about the existence of the *Shiji*." Later in the Tang Dynasty, more importance was attached to the *Shiji* and many versions emerged. As a result of the "Ancient Text Movement" against the *Pianti* Style, the *Shiji* became popular. However,

"史家之绝唱，无韵之离骚"，这是鲁迅在《汉文学史纲要》中对《史记》所作的确切评语，是对《史记》的极大褒赞。

从史学来说，《史记》是集大成的著作。思想文化的许多领域，包括天文、地理、哲学、军事、文学等等，它都涉及到了，并作出了不小的贡献。《史记》继承并发扬了古代良史不虚美、不隐恶的优良传统，也可以作为后世史书的楷模。宋代史学家郑樵曾评论说："百代以下，史官不能易其法，学者不能舍其书。"清代史学家赵翼也称之为"史家之极则"，当然，他们所强调的只是《史记》所创造的体例，而不可能深入地发掘《史记》的思想意义。司马迁写作《史记》，那种"究天人之际，通古今之变，成一家之言"的气魄，那种"原始察终，见盛观衰"的发展变化的观点，那种不以成败论人的勇气，都是封建时代的史学家难以达到的。《史记》行世之后，便有一些人搜辑故事替他作续篇，"然多鄙俗，不足以踵继其书"，后来也都散佚了。东汉初，班彪接《史记》之后，作《史记后传》六十五篇，这成了其子班固编写《汉书》的基础。班固的《汉书》是《史记》之后很有影响的著作。它的体例基本沿袭《史记》，只是将"世家"并入了列传，将"书"改称"志"。《汉书》是断代史，只写西汉王朝一代的历史，武帝以前的文字基本采用《史记》。可是，班固的思想比较保守，缺乏批判精神。《汉书》的文学技巧也不及《史记》，语言则倾向于对偶。由于统治阶级的提倡和六朝以来盛行骈体文的缘故，在相当一段时间内，《汉书》的影响远超过《史记》，所谓"汉晋名贤未知见重"，正说明《史记》颇被那个时期士大夫冷落的情况。唐代，人们比较重视《史记》，出现了多种注本。尤其在"古文运动"反对骈体文之后，《史记》的文章更被看重。然而，就过去的各种史书来看，它们所能继承《史记》的，主要是它的体例和

all that was left for later historic books was the style of the *Shiji*, some skills at the use of words, and also the tradition of "no boasting and no covering up." It is hard to find the same kind of strong criticism that exists in the historical works of Sima Qian. Sima Qian was a product of his times, and such an historian who can not reappear in a different society. When a great comet appears in the sky, it leaves a long-lasting impression.

From a literary perspective, the influence of the *Shiji* is also long-lasting. The *Shiji* recorded the history of the times based on facts. Sima Qian's artistic approach did not alter the truth itself. We can say the *Shiji* is realistic in nature. The historical period that the *Shiji* covered, especially the Period of the Warring States and the war between the Chu and the Han, was a heroic period. Figures in this period were all legendary. Sima Qian added his own idea when describing the historical figures, and he glorified some. At the same time, he inserted more passion into his description. In a way, the *Shiji* was very romantic. The combination of realism and romanticism contributed to the high status the *Shiji* enjoyed in the literary world.

Poets in the past who wanted to search for historic facts would turn to the *Shiji* as it provided them with lots of material and inspiration. Tao Yuanming, a great poet, who wrote "The Praise of Jing Ke," rewrote the story of Jing Ke, the assassin, in a poem. The feelings in the words he wrote echoed those of Sima Qian. For example, "The cold wind is gradually dying down and the cold waves are moving." "Even though the assassin has died, for a thousand years, we will remember what he did." The great poet Li Bai of the Tang Dynasty, who also had the spirits like that of those gallant citizens, also admired them. In his poems, Li Bai expressed his wish to follow the example of Lu Zhonglian. Li Bai also admired Zhang Liang's gallant acts and highly spiritual wisdom that made him use up all of his money but not for his own family. Li Bai was a great scholar but was not appreciated by the authority. He felt the world was unfair and he wrote how Han Xin and Jia Yi were treated, "The city of the Huai Yin all laughed at Han Xin while ministers of the Han Dynasty all hated Jia Yi." From Li Bai's examples we can learn that a great

某些文字技巧，"不虚美，不隐恶"的精神作为一种历史的回响，也多少起过一些作用。《史记》中卓越的史识，强烈的批判精神，在后来的史书中便难以找到了。司马迁毕竟是他那个特定时代的产儿，是不可能重复出现的。彗星经天，留给人们的是长久的憧憬。

从文学角度来说，《史记》的影响则十分深远。《史记》的传记文学是以历史事实为依据的，作者的艺术加工，也是按照生活本来的面貌来表现的。因此，可以说《史记》具有强烈的现实主义精神。可是《史记》所反映的时代——其中最突出的是战国和楚汉战争时代，可以说是一个"英雄时代"。这时代的一些人物，颇具传奇色彩，再加上司马迁描绘这些人物时寄托了自己的理想，更为这些人物增添了光辉。同时其文章也写得奔腾变幻、热情洋溢。因此，《史记》又具有相当浓厚的积极浪漫主义精神。现实主义精神和积极浪漫主义精神，奠立了《史记》在文学史上的崇高地位。

过去时代的诗人往往是向历史寻找诗情的，《史记》则为他们提供了丰富的资料和深刻的启示。例如陶渊明曾写过《咏荆轲》，将《刺客列传》中的荆轲故事，用诗的形式再创造出来，"萧萧哀风逝，淡淡寒波生"，"其人虽已没，千载有余情"。这些句子表现了诗人对荆轲的钦慕和与司马迁的共鸣。有任侠精神的李白，对《史记》中的某些充满传奇性的豪侠人物更是无限倾倒。在不少诗篇中，他对鲁仲连一再表示了仰慕以至效法的意思。在李白心目中，张良也是一个受崇拜的对象。他特别欣赏张良"破产不为家"那种毁家纾难的任侠精神和极高超的才智。李白怀才不遇，深感世事的不平，于是便引韩信、贾谊为同调，写出"淮阴市井笑韩信，汉朝公卿忌贾生"的诗句。以上这些例子可以说明，像李白这样伟大的诗人，不仅从《史

poet like him drew on material from the *Shiji*, and he truly followed the spirit of Sima Qian in that he criticised and praised the matters recorded in the *Shiji*. Many other accomplished poets, especially those romantic ones, also benefited from the spirit of the *Shiji*, and their thoughts all echoed those of Sima Qian.

In terms of essay writing, the *Shiji*'s influence is complex. After Han Yu and Liu Zongyuan promoted the "Ancient Text Movement," the writing style of the *Shiji* became popular. Both men promoted the idea that scholars should learn from the *Shiji*. From what Han Yu wrote, we can see he had been influenced by the *Shiji*. In "The Biography of Zhang Zhongcheng," Han Yu wrote about how Nan Jiyun broke the army defence and rushed to Helan Jinming for help. Helan refused. Qiyun drew his bow and shot an arrow at the top of a pagoda and vowed, "After destroying the enemies, I will definitely come and kill Helan. My arrow will be the proof of what I have just said. This story was quite famous in the region. Han Yu retold the stories in great detail. He also provided his own comments while describing the events. All these were similar to the style of the *Shiji*. Essayists of the Tang and Song dynasties all attached great importance to the *Shiji*. Essayists and critics after the Ming Dynasty also discussed and commented on the writing style of the *Shiji*, and while their views may not have been perfect, they did provide some views of acceptable quality. Liu Dakui, a representative figure of the Tongcheng School, said, "To record an event and to express one's feelings, this is what the *Shiji* did." Many successful biographical essays used a similar approach.

Some dramatic chapters in the *Shiji* became materials for the creation of novels and dramas later on. Examples can be seen in the story books written in the Ming and the Qing dynasties, such as *The Stories of States in the Eastern Zhou Period, Stories of Western Han* and *Stories of Sun Pang*, all adopted contents of the *Shiji*. Some other texts, such as *The Stories of Wu Zixu, The Stories of General Wang Ling of the Han, The Stories of Ji Bu's Capture* and *The Stories of Li Ling*, all used resources of the *Shiji*, also. Stories in the Ming Dynasty, such as *The Flying General Li Guang of the Han Dynasty* and *The Zhuo Wenjun Wisely Learnt Sima Xiangru*, were based on stories in the *Shiji*. Besides, out of 132 Yuan Operas, 16 stories came from the *Shiji*. Examples include, *The Orphan of the Zhao*, written by Ji Junxiang; *Wu Zixu's Revenge*, written by Li Shouqing; *Xiao He Chases Han Xin*, written by Jin Renjie and *The Complete Jade Returning to Zhao*, by Gao Wenxiu. Some operas written in the Ming Dynasty include *The Rinsing of Silk*, written by Liang Chenyu; *The Stealing of a Tally*, written by Zhang Fengyi; *The Heart for Zithers*, written by Sun You; and *The Story of the Princess*, written by Shen Cai. In Beijing opera

记》中取得素材，而且也像《史记》一样地是非褒贬，有歌颂也有批判，真正继承了司马迁的精神。李白只是一个突出的例子，可以说历代有成就的诗人，尤其是具有积极浪漫主义精神的诗人，无不受到《史记》精神的影响，并与司马迁有着思想上的共鸣。

在散文方面，《史记》的影响较为复杂。从韩愈、柳宗元等提倡古文运动以后，对于《史记》笔法的学习便较普遍。韩、柳都讲过要学习《史记》文章的话。从其创作实践来看，确实从《史记》中得到不少助力。如韩愈的《张中丞传后序》，写南霁云冲出重围向贺兰进明求救，贺兰不允，霁云一箭射中塔顶以明誓："吾归破贼，必灭贺兰，此矢所以志也。"这段故事是父老相传的，韩愈将它写进文章，倍觉生动。这篇文章通过生动的细节和模仿人物口吻来刻画人物；采用夹叙夹议的方式表达作者的主观感情……凡此种种都和《史记》有很多相似之处。唐宋散文家一般都重视向《史记》学习。明代以后许多散文家、评点家对《史记》的写作方法作了枝枝节节的探讨、评论。他们的观点不免穿凿、琐碎，但也还包含了一些可取的意见。如桐城派代表人物刘大櫆所说"即事以寓情，《史记》之文也"，便指出了《史记》传记文学的主要特点。文学史上许多写得成功的传记体散文，无不是充分体现了这样一个特点。

《史记》的纪传中，有一些情节极生动、很富戏剧性的篇章，为后世的小说、戏剧创作提供了丰富的素材。就小说来看，明清的历史演义像《东周列国志》、《西汉演义》、《孙庞演义》等，参考了《史记》是不用说了。唐代变文，如《伍子胥变文》、《汉将王陵变》、《捉季布传文》、《李陵变文》等，也显然从《史记》中有所取材。明人平话像《汉李广世号飞将军》、《卓文君慧眼识相如》等，其素材也来源于《史记》。就戏剧来看，

there are numerous famous dramas coming from the *Shiji*. Examples are *The Pass of Wenzhao (Wenzhaoguan)*, *The King Chu Bidding Farewell to His Concubine*, *The Chase for Han Xin*, which are all famous ones loved by the audience. The *Shiji* has influenced not only the content of novels and dramas of later generations, but also the spirit and writing style. For example, the author of *Strange Tales from the Chat House* claimed that he wrote the book in order to vent his anger. We can see that the author did learn from Sima Qian and the comments at the end of each story mirror the "Postface" written by Sima Qian.

Many commentaries were written on the *Shiji*. If all those commentaries were put together, a fairly big library would need to be built to accommodate them. I'd like to introduce a few common books here.

1. *Collected Annotations of the* Shiji, by Pei Yin, Song Dynasty; *The Shiji Roman-a-clef*, by Sima Zhen, Tang Dynasty; *The True Meaning of the* Shiji, by Zhang Shoujie, Tang Dynasty. These three books were independently written but were anthologised in the Song Dynasty under the title of "the Three Commentaries." This is a very popular version. The Zhonghua Book Company's new version with new format punctuations is useful for readers.

2. *A Collection of Commentaries of the* Shiji, by Ling Zhilong, Ming Dynasty. This book collects all commentaries on the *Shiji* and can be easily used as an index.

3. *Questions in the* Shiji, by Liang Yusheng, Qing Dynasty. The author investigated the facts recorded in the *Shiji*.

4. In Japan, there are *The Study of the Commentaries on the* Shiji, by Takigawa Kametaro; and also *The Amendments on a Study of the Commentaries on the* Shiji, by Mizusawa Toshitada. Takigawa's collection is a good guide to be used.

There are also many modern studies on the *Shiji* and many new methods of research have been created. The information can be easily accessed and I will not be introducing these studies here.

In summary, the *Shiji* is very influential in many ways. It is a spiritual

现存一百三十二种元剧，采取《史记》故事的便有十六种。其中较有名的如纪君祥的《赵氏孤儿》，李寿卿的《伍员吹箫》，金仁杰的《萧何追韩信》，高文秀的《完璧归赵》。明代传奇中则有梁辰鱼的《浣纱记》，张凤翼的《窃符记》，孙柚的《琴心记》，沈采的《千金记》等作品。京剧中取材自《史记》的极多，像《文昭关》、《霸王别姬》、《追韩信》等都是人们熟知的剧目。当然，《史记》给予后世小说戏剧的影响，绝不限于提供素材，在精神上和写作方法上则更有着广泛的影响。如《聊斋志异》，作者自称为"抒孤愤"之作，在精神上文笔上都仿效着《史记》，其每篇后面异史氏的评语，也分明由"太史公曰"脱胎出来。

随着《史记》流传的广泛，为它作注，对它进行研究的也多了。这方面的著作如果集中起来，便可以建立一个不小的图书馆。我在这里，只打算提出几种通用的书，以供参考。

（一）刘宋裴骃《史记集解》，唐司马贞《史记索隐》，唐张守节《史记正义》。这三部书原来各自独立，宋代合刻在一起，称三家注，成为最通行的注本。现有中华书局出版的标点本，最便利用。

（二）明凌稚隆编《史记评林》。此书汇集历代评论《史记》的材料，颇便于翻检。

（三）清梁玉绳《史记志疑》。此书对书中所记史实，作了详细的考辨。

（四）日本泷川龟太郎《史记会注考证》及水泽利忠《史记会注考证校补》。泷川氏的书汇集了许多考证资料，可当指南之用。

现代人研究《史记》，开辟了很多新路子，著述比较多，也较易得到，就不列举了。

treasure for humanity and its influence has gone beyond its birth place—China. Many chapters have been translated into other languages and foreign researchers have been working on them. In 1956, Sima Qian was referred to as one of the World's Cultural Celebrities. The widespread interest and acclaim demonstrate that the *Shiji* is considered the essence of traditional Chinese culture, and that it is a very valuable cultural heritage. To safeguard this heritage and maintain its glory is the task for all of us.

　　总之，《史记》的影响是巨大的，多方面的。作为人类宝贵的精神财富，它的影响更已越出了诞生它的中华大地。其中的一些篇章早被译成多种外语，并且国外也有不少著名的研究者。1956年司马迁被列为世界文化名人，受到各国人民的纪念。这一切都说明，司马迁的《史记》是我国传统文化中民主性的精华，是宝贵的文化遗产，继承这份文化遗产，让它不断发出新的光辉，正是我们的责任。

汉代雕塑"马踏飞燕"
Sculpture of the Han Dynasty "the Galloping Horse with Its Right Hind Foot on a Flying Swallow"

Translators' Notes

Sima Qian (135 B.C.— 86 B.C.) is the most influential and respected imperial historian in China. His work *Shiji* (*Records of the Grand Historian of China*) is acknowledged by many Chinese to be the richest and most complex book recording the first three thousand years of history up to the Han Dynasty.

The book *Sima Qian* provides readers with a brief history of the grand historian and his talent as a writer. Sima Qian is from a historian's family. His own life experience as court astrologer and Palace Attendant, and opportunities to travel broadly to most places in ancient China allowed him to obtain first hand information that enabled him to revisit the written history and collect new materials to rewrite history. Sima Qian had a complex life with dramatic ups and downs. He was imprisoned due to the fact that he bravely spoke up to protect the unfairly persecuted general. Fighting against the tragedy he pulled himself together and completed the *Shiji*. The trajectory of his life spelt the complexity of the politics and nature of China's feudal society. By reading the book *Sima Qian* one can taste the long, vivid and complex history of Chinese feudal society. The 130-chapter *Shiji* is a gold mine of ancient Chinese history. It not only provides readers with the major historians, and social events, but also the social culture shaped by these figures and events. Sima Qian's *Shiji* is a splendid literature to readers in China and worldwide. Like Samual Johnson is the father of English literature and the dictionary, Sima Qian is the father of China's history and literature. He set the standard and model for recording Chinese history for later historiographers.

The title of Sima Qian's book, *Shiji*, has been translated into different English versions. The most frequently used titles are "Records of the Grand Historian of China" by Watson and the "Grand Scribe's Records" by William H. Nienhauser Jr. In our translation, we use the Chinese Pinyin system for the title—*Shiji*. The word *shi* means history and *ji* means record. As for the translation of the book *Sima Qian*, in order to better meet western readers' need, we adopt the principle of maintaining the meaning of the book rather than its literal form.

图书在版编目(CIP)数据

司马迁/郭维森著；(澳)杨国生，(澳)爱博译
.—南京：南京大学出版社，2010.7
(中国思想家评传简明读本：中英文版)
ISBN 978-7-305-07294-9

Ⅰ.①司…　Ⅱ.①郭…②杨…③爱…　Ⅲ.①司马迁
(前145～前90)—评传—汉、英　Ⅳ.①K825.81

中国版本图书馆CIP数据核字(2010)第145658号

出版发行　南京大学出版社
社　　址　南京汉口路22号　邮　编　210093
网　　址　http://www.NjupCo.com
出版人　左　健

丛 书 名　《中国思想家评传》简明读本(中英文版)
书　　名　司马迁
著　　者　郭维森
译　　者　Guosheng Yang Chen, Bo Ai
审　　读　张　静
责任编辑　芮逸敏　　　　编辑热线　025-83593962

照　　排　江苏凤凰制版印务中心
印　　刷　南京大众新科技印刷有限公司
开　　本　787×1092　1/16　印张 10.75　字数 189千
版　　次　2010年7月第1版　2010年7月第1次印刷
ISBN 978-7-305-07294-9
定　　价　23.00元

发行热线　025-83594756　83686452
电子邮箱　Press@NjupCo.com
　　　　　Sales@NjupCo.com（市场部）